An
HISTORICAL ESSAY

Endeavoring a Probability

That the

LANGUAGE

Of the Empire of

CHINA

is the

Primitive

LANGUAGE.

Constanter

By *John Webb* of *Butleigh* in the
County of *Somerset* Esquire.

LONDON,
Printed for *Nath. Brook,* at the *Angel*
in *Gresham* Colledge. 1669.
Lond. Dec. 1670

Licenſed

By Authority.

TO
THE MOST SACRED
MAJESTY
OF

CHARLES
The Second.

SIR,

NEW DISCOVE-
RIES *make the Lives
of* PRINCES *famous;
Their* POSTERITY
powerful; Their Subjects rich.
Most prudently therefore doth
YOUR MAJESTY vouch-
safe to encourage them. Which raif-
eth a Spirit in the Hearts of Your
People to profecute the fame. It being fully verified in Your Majefty,
what was faid unto that famous Em-

A 2   perour

The Epistle

perour of C H I N A, HIAVOUUS,
The vertue of a KING is like
the Wind, his Subjects like
Corn, which incline all to that
part, whereunto they are moved
by the Wind.

This E S S A Y *in all humble
submission invokes* Y O U R R O Y-
A L Protection, *it pretends to advance the* D I S C O V E R Y *of that*
G O L D E N-M I N E *of* Learning,
which from all A N T I Q U I T Y
hath lain concealed in the P R I M I-
T I V E T O N G U E ; *whether*
Religion, *Famous* Examples *of the*
Wisedom *of* Old, *Politique* Rules
*for Government, or what ever else ad-
vantageous to* Mankind *be respected.
And wherein no doubt, so great My-
steries are involved, as nothing
hitherto in all the* Learning *of the
World can either excel or equal.*

Hence *it is, that so many* Wri-
ters, in almost all Ages *since the*
Birth

Birth of CHRIST *have one way or other treated thereof : some asserting the* Teutonique *to be it ; some the* Samaritan *; others the* Phænician *; divers* Churchmen *pleading as well for the* Chaldæan, *as* Hebrew. *With what success I question not; my intention being, not to dispute what in* Possibility *cannot, but what in* probability *may be the* First Speech. *Neither is it my purpose with others to insist on* vulgar Traditions, *or* licentious *Etymologies of* Words; *weak and frail Foundations to support such a* Weight, *but fix my* Basis *upon* Sacred Truth, *and credible* History. *Scripture teacheth, that the whole* Earth *was of one* Language *until the* Conspiracy *at* BABEL; *History informs that* CHINA *was peopled, whilst the* Earth *was so of one* Language, *and before that Conspiracy.* Scripture *teacheth that*

the *Judgment* of Confusion *of*
Tongues, *fell upon those only that
were at* BABEL: History *informs, that the* CHINOIS *being fully setled before, were not
there* ; *And moreover that the same*
LANGUAGE *and* CHA-
RACTER S *which long preceding
that* Confusion *they used, are in
use with them at this very* DAY;
whether the Hebrew, or Greek
Chronology *be consulted.*

The Scripture *is infallible, my*
principal Authors, *fide Sacerdotum
datâ, profess* Integrity, *as having
of very late* Daies, *by long study
compiled the* History *of* CHINA,
from the Antient Records *thereof,
ever since the time of* NOAH. The
Foundation *then not failing, my*
Superstructure *most probably stands,
So much the firmer*; *as that how
valid soever transient* Words *are,
written* Records *be of far more certain*

AN ESSAY

Towards the

PRIMITIVE

Language.

BY what manner of Policy, the severall Nations and People of the world were governed before the Flood, no certain memory is remaining, nor any record to which we may give juſt credit, extant; either of the wars or peace, or other actions that were then performed. But that they had Kings, Rulers, and ſet Forms of Government, undertook noble Enterpriſes, made Invaſions, ſubdued Countries, managed with great advice the affairs of war, and atchieved many things worthy of admiration, there is no cauſe to doubt. For, their exceeding long lives, having, to their ſtrength of body, added the experience of eight hundred or nine hundred years, muſt neceſſarily increaſe their wiſe-

B

doms

dome and conduct, and render their undertakings (had they been communicated to posterity) far more excellent, than whatever can be related of after-times.

And though *Moses* passeth over this first Age in so short a narrative as seven brief chapters; and, writing an history of and for the Church, mentioneth no farther, the affairs and nations of the world, than was meet for the Church, that of the *Israelites* especially, to know, according as it was likely they should have then, or after, more or less to doe with them; much nevertheless may be collected from him in relation to the condition of that time. For, we find that the men of those days were mighty and famous; his words *Gen.* 6. *v.* 4. being, *They were mighty men, which were of old men of renown.* We may stile them *Hero's*, such as either through their valour brought almost impossible and admirable attempts to an unexpected and desired issue; or such as by their vertue were the Authors of profitable Arts and Sciences, and reduced Mankind to civil and sociable conversation.

But it is not to be denied, that then there were mighty men in regard of bodily stature also; whom the Scripture calleth from their greatness and terribleness *Rephaim* and *Emim*, from their pride *Anakim*; from their strength *Gibborim* in *Gibborim*; from their Tyranny *Nephilim*; from their naughtiness *Zamzummim*; such were *Og* and *Goliah* after the Flood. But howsoever the bodies of these men were composed, certain it is, that before the Deluge, they divided

(as

(as we by the *Civil* Law are now wont to doe) their goods amongſt their children; aſſigning their Real eſtates to the eldeſt of their ſons, and their Perſonal to the younger. For, *Adam* gave unto *Cain* Lands to Till, unto *Abel* Sheep to Feed.

Poſterity being multiplied, they fell immediately to the building of Cities, fortifying of Caſtles, driving of Cattle, committing of Slaughters, and whatever elſe the intereſt of their wilfulneſs perſwaded them unto; Theſe things being done by them as well for neceſſary habitation, as for ſtrength and ſafety to ſecure themſelves, and oppreſs others. That they did build Cities, no doubt is to be made; for if *Jabal* was the firſt that dwelt in Tents, Where ſhould the reſt dwell, ſaith *Heylin*, but in Citties, Towns, or Villages? And that the firſt of Cities was built by *Cain*, as alſo that he called it after the name of his Son *Enoch*, the Scripture teacheth *Gen* 4. *v.* 17. which was either erected by him, to croſs that curſe of his wandring to and fro; or to arme him againſt others, whom his guilty conſcience cauſed him to feare; or to be a receptacle and ſtorehouſe of thoſe ſpoiles, which by force and violence, *Joſephus* tells us, he took from others, when the earth was barren to him, and would afford him nothing. Probable it is, that the City was called *Enoch*, becauſe, the curſe not ſuffering the Father to ſtay in any place, he was enforced to commit an haſty inheritance to his ſon, and leave him to finiſh and govern the ſame.

To this manner of life, in regard of general

Joſ. Anti. Judd.lib. 1l c. 3.

use, several Arts were invented ; *One* finds out
the making of Tents, in which leading a wandring life, his robberies might be the more concealed, and his flocks and heards the better fed.
Another the forging of iron usefull for the making of arms, and weapons of war ; and what
else they could of that kind. *Another,* Musique:
whereby the affections being enflamed, they
were stirred up unto those things, in which
they placed their greatest happiness. So that
as this race of men, acted all things not by
reason, but lust ; frequent contentions, private
quarrels, and open war, could not but of necessity arise amongst them : and, though they
might be well enough able from themselves to
defend themselves ; the other party, the children of *Seth* nevertheless lived no more safely
amongst them, than silly sheep amongst raging
wolves.

Idem c.4.　They were as great Idolaters, if not greater
then those of the after-age to which they gave
example ; for, degenerating, saith *Josephus,* from
the ancient institutions of their fore-fathers,
they neither observed the service of God, nor
humane Laws. But were fierce and cruel, full
of Injustice, Oppression, Murther, Rapine, Pride
and Ambition, all concomitants of war, and
presages of ruine to insue. Which Ambition
and Pride had, as it seemeth, a very early influence upon the Leaders of the succeeding Age,
otherwise they could not possibly have imagined
that they should make themselves a name, by
the building of such a work at *Babel,* as they en-
terprised to erect ; nor so soon have known
what

what war meant, as that, ere they were well
warme in their new feats, to invade one another. For, the iſſues of *Aſſur*, and the iſſues of
Cham, ſaith Sir *W. Raleigh*, fell inſtantly at con-
tention for the Empire of the Eaſt.

As for fruits of Peace, they had Theology, 144.
Propheſie, Aſtronomy, Aſtrology; had Weights
and Meaſures ; and *Cain*, as *Joſephus* relates,
firſt aſſigned proprieties in poſſeſſion of Land, before as common as the Ayre and Light: therefore *Meum* and *Tuum* was even in thoſe times.
Concerning their manner of diet: many are of
opinion, that they eat no fleſh, but fed on ve-
getable aliments, thoſe at the leaſt of the race
of *Seth*, who obeyed the command of God. And
this may be collected from the very Text, *Behold, I have given you every hearb-bearing ſeed,
which is upon the face of all the earth; and every
tree, in thee which is the fruit of a tree yielding ſeed
to you, it ſhall be for meat ; Gen. 1. v. 29.* which
plainly ſheweth, they were utterly prohibited
the eating of fleſh. Neither doe we read, that
this prohibition was taken off, till immediately
after the deſcent of *Noah* from the Ark, when
either, becauſe the Deluge had impaired or in-
firmed the nature of vegetables, God giving
him an augmentation of his words, ſaid, *Every
moving thing that liveth ſhall be meat for you ; even
as the green hearb have I given you all things, Gen.
9. v. 3.* And though it may be ſuppoſed, the firſt
men would not keep ſheep, except they made
food of them; very learned expoſitors will tell
us that it was partly for their skins, with which
they clothed themſelves ; partly for their milk,

Sir *Walt.*
Ra. Hiſt.
par.1.pa.
144.

with

with which they suftained them, and partly for
Dr. T.Br.
in Pseud.
Epid.l.3.p.
141.
offerings which they sacrificed unto God. As
Dr. *Brown* in his *Pseudodoxia Epidemica* hath delivered.

They enjoyed the use of Letters: for *Josephus*
attesteth, that *Adam* having prophesied two u-
niversal Destructions, one by fire, another by
water, his posterity erected two pillars, one of
brick, another of stone, in both which they writ
their inventions of Astronomy. But, notwithstanding he thus witnesseth, yet whether those
of *Adams* posterity that erected the same pillars
invented the Letters they engraved on them,
he saith not: whereby we may conjecture, that,
admitting the engravements were made be *Seth*
or *Enoch*, the Characters nevertheless were
more ancient, and by some other found out; of
which haply we shall have somewhat more to
say. However, of these Epigraphs the Scripture
seemeth not to be altogether silent; for we read,
*Judg. 3. v. 26. And Ehud escaped while they tar-
ried, and passed beyond the Quarries, and escaped
unto Seirath.* Now *Isi. Vossius* tells us, that
Is. Voss. de
Ætat.
mun.p.35.
this Translation receding from the true signification of the Hebrew word, puts Quarries for
Sculptures. But the Seventy have rightly rendred it τὰ γλυπτὰ; for there, saith he, was that
stony Pillar which the *Hebrews* believe *Seth* set
up, as *Josephus* alleadgeth, who writes that
even in his time the same Pillar remained in a
place called *Syriada*.

Some ascribe the invention of Astronomy to
Seth, as also the first naming of the seven Planets: Others to *Enoch*, who, they say, much fur-
thered

lions. So that either that firſt age was as much
or more ſubject to Plagues, Peſtilences, Fa-
mines, Wars, Loſſes, and Calamities, as after-
times; or elſe, either the world could not contain ſuch prodigious multitudes; or they muſt
devoure one another for want of food and habitations. For, granting the Terreſtrial Globe
to be all habitable Earth, no Seas intervening
and dividing it into twelve equall parts; it
will be found, allotting to each diviſion two
hundred and fifty millions of people, that
three thouſand millions will fully plant the
ſame, and make it more wonderfully populous
than this extream part of *Aſia*, whereof we
are to treat. But being, ſcarcely the one half
of it only is habitable, and Sea poſſeſſeth the
reſt; fifteen hundred millions will more than
enough ſuffice: Whereby it is demonſtrable,
that, if for ſetling of Plantations multitudes of
people be requirable, the whole Earth was
throughly planted before the Flood. But how
innumerable ſoever their numbers appear to be,
by the juſt judgement of God upon them for
their manifold offences, they were, by the firſt
of the univerſall deſtructions; *Water*, all deſtroyed.

The Scripture is very manifeſt and plain
herein, *And behold, I, even I* (ſaith the Lord)
*doe bring a flood of waters upon the earth, to de-
ſtroy all fleſh, wherein is the breath of life, from
under Heaven, and every thing that is in the
Earth ſhall die,* Gen. 6. v. 17. Againe, Gen. 7.
v. 19. *And the waters prevailed exceedingly upon
the Earth, and all the high hills that were under
                                        the*

the whole Heaven were covered. Now this drowning of the world, hath not been quite drown'd
in the world; for, even by prophane Authors
it is remembred. To omit others, *Lucian* in
his *Dea Syria* relateth the opinion of the *Hiera-
politans*, but a little corrupted from the narra-
tion of *Moses*; so plainly doth he attribute to
his *Deucalion* the Ark, the resort and safeguard
of the lyons, bores, serpents, and beasts; the repair-
ing of the world after this drowning thereof,
which he ascribeth to the perjury, cruelty, and o-
ther abominations of the former people. *Berosus*
not as in *Amnius* that brat of a Monk, but as
in *Abydenus* that ancient Historian, cited by

Sir *W. Ra.*
hist. par. I.
p. 88.

Eusebius, as I find in Sir *W. Raleigh*, affirmeth,
that *Saturn* gave warning to *Sisithrus* of this
Deluge, and willed him to prepare a great Vessel or ship, wherein to put convenient food, and
to save himself with his kindred and acquain-
tance; which he builded, of length five furlongs, and of bredth two. After the retiring
of the waters, he sent out a Bird which returned; after a few days he sent her forth again,

Plut: de a-
nim. com-
parat.

which returned with her feet bemired; and being sent out the third time came no more. *Plutarch* also hath written of this Dove, sent by *Deucalion* out of the Ark, which returning was a sign
of tempest; and flying forth, of faire weather.

Simler.
Ortel.
Fracastor.
apud Meu:
Cent.

At *Berne* in *Switzerland* in the year 1460. in
a Mine from whence they drew out Metal-Ore,
at fifty fathom deep, a ship was digged up, in
which were forty eight carcases of men, with
Merchants goods: At *Shotesham* in *Norfolk*
within the lands of Sir *William Doyle* Knight,

in

misus, and *Caucasus,* the general name of *Taurus,* so was *Ararat* the general name which *Moses* gave them, the diversity of appellations no otherwise growing, than by their dividing and bordering divers Regions, and divers Countries. As in like manner we do call that, that doth generally go by the name of the *Mediterranean* Sea, sometimes the *Tyrrhene, Ionian, Adriatique,* and *Ægean* ; sometimes the *Hellespont, Pontus, Propontis,* and *Bosphorus,* according to the several Countries it passeth by, and the several Coasts it washeth. And therefore seeing that *Moses* teacheth us, that all those people, which under the conduct of *Nimrod* entred the Valley of *Shinaar,* came from the East, *And as they went from the East, they found a plain in the land of Shinaar, and there they abode,* Gen. 11. v. 2. We may I suppose, saith he, without controversie resolve, that the Ark of *Noah* rested and took ground upon those Mountains of *Taurus,* or *Ararat,* as *Moses* calleth them, which lye Eastward from *Shinaar,* between East-*India* and *Scythia* ; and not on those Mountains of the North-west, betwixt *Mesopotamia,* and *Armenia major,* as *Berosus* first faigned, and most Writers, following him have since mistaken.

  Goropius Becanus in his *Indo-Scythia* maintains, that the Ark rested on the top of Mount *Caucasus,* in the confines of *Tartaria, Persia,* and *India,* using many arguments for his opinion ; as amongst others the exceeding populousness of the Eastern Countries, but relying principally upon the aforesaid Text of Scripture. With him

Gor. Bec. Indof. p. 473.

Heylin

Heyl.Cosm.
Pag. 7.
Heylin joynes issue; saying, 'If then they came
'from the East to the land of *Shinaar*, as the
'Text saith plainly that they did, it might well
'be, that they came from those parts of *Asia*;
'on the South of *Caucasus*, which lye East from
'*Shinaar*, though somewhat bending into the
'North, impossible they should come from the
'*Gordiæan* Mountains in the greater *Armenia*,
'which lye not onely full North from *Shi-*
'*naar*, but many degrees unto the West.

The first thing mentioned in Scripture, that
Noah did after his coming forth of the Ark,
having sacrificed and returned thanks to God
for his deliverance, was, to Till the Ground and
Plant. *And Noah began to be an Husbandman,
and he planted a Vineyard, Gen. 9. v. 20.* And manifest it is, that he travailed not far to seek out
the Vine, for the Plantation thereof is remembred, before he entred into any counsel, how to
dispose of the World amongst his children. In
regard whereof many are of opinion, that *Noah*
seated himself in the East, in or near to the
place, where he first went forth of the Ark, and
that he never came to *Shinaar* at all. For he was
too principall a person to be either forgotten or
Sir Wal.
Ral.hist,
par. 1. pag.
158.
neglected, had he removed with *Nimrod* thither. And it is no where found, saith. Sir *W.*
Raleigh, that *Noah* himself came with this Troop
to *Babylon*, no mention at all being made of him
(the years of his life excepted) in the succeeding
story of the *Hebrews*, nor that *Sem*, or any
of the Sons of *Noah's* own body, was in this
disobedient company, or among the builders of
Id. 144.
Babel. Therefore it is very probable that *Noah*
                                        taking

taking up his reft, not far from the place where
the Ark grounded, firft inhabited *India*, and had
well peopled all thofe parts, which lay neereft to
him, before he fent *Nimrod*, and his followers
forth upon new difcoveries. Hence the fame Author telleth us alfo, that from the Eaft came
the firft knowledge of all things, and that the
Eaft parts of the world were the firft civilized,
having *Noah* himfelf for an Inftructer, whereby the farther Eaft to this day, the more
Civil, the farther Weft the more Savage.

Id. p. 109.

　In confirmation hereof *Heylin* likewife declares, that Sir *W. Raleigh* pleads the point exceeding ftrongly, that it muft needs be, that
Noah was fetled in the Eaft, and had well
peopled all thofe parts which lay neareft to
him, before he fent *Nimrod* and his Troop a-
broad to fearch for other habitations. And after having very ftudioufly difcourfed of the feveral generations, and difperfions of the Sons of
Noah, fo far forth as their names are regiftred
in holy Scripture to be the Heads and Leaders
of thofe feveral Tribes, which joyned together
in the defign for the building of *Babel*, and afterwards difperfed themfelves, he proceedeth,
faying, But that no more than thefe (I mean,
faith he, heads of Families) defcended in fo long
a time from the loines of *Noah*, that they fhould
have towards the new peopling of the world in
an hundred years (for fo long time it muft be
at leaft from the Flood, to the building of *Babel*,) no more than fixteen Sons in all, and ten
of thofe fixte goe childlefs to the grave, is not
a thing to be imagined. Nor is it to be thought

*Heyl. Cof n.
p. 16, 17.*

C 3　　　　　that

that all the people which were born since the
flood till then, could meet together at one
place as by inspiration ; or being met could
joyne together in a work of so little profit; or
that if *Noah* or *Sem* had been there amongst
them, they would not have diswaded them from
that foolish enterprise. And therefore I should
rather be of their opinion which think, that
Noah fixed himself in those parts, which lay
neerest to the place where the Ark took land,
and having planted as far Eastward as he thought
convenient, sent out the surplusage of his people,
under the conduct of one or more of these Un-
dertakers, directing them perhaps to the land of
Shinaar, where himself had dwelt before the
flood. For, in regard there is none of those,
though most diligent men, who have written
of the Plantations of the world upon this dif-
persion, that either speak of any Nations planted by *Noah* himself, or *Sem* and *Japhet*, or of
their setling in the Colonies of any one of their
Descendents ; it is to me saith *Heylin* again, a
very strong argument, that they came not with
the rest to the Plains of *Shinaar*, but tarried still
in those habitations, wherein God had planted
them.

Purch. Pil-
grimage,
lib. 1. p. 67. *Purchas* thinks, that before the flood *Noah* lived in *Syria* (which probably his Author might
mistake for *Serica*) but whether there, or in the
land of *Shinaar*, or wheresoever else; *Josephus*
affirms, that he forsook his native Country, and
with his Wife and Family travailed into another Region, where he built the Ark. Now,
though what became of him, or w.. ther he removed

moved is uncertain. Neverthele‍ſs it is mo‍ſt
‍ſure, ‍ſaith. *Willet,* that he neither joyned with
Nimrod, nor his company, nor ever ingaged
with them ; and although the Scripture maketh no mention of the re‍ſt of his Acts, yet no
doubt is to be made, but that he exerci‍ſed him-
‍ſelf in Planting of Religion, and doing mo‍ſt excellent works for the benefit of Mankind, of
which *Mo‍ſes* omitteth to ‍ſpeak, as al‍ſo of the
proceedings of the Godly ‍ſucceeding Fathers,
becau‍ſe he ha‍ſteth to the ‍ſtory of *Abraham.*

A. Willet in Gen. 8. *&* 11

That *Noah* ‍ſtaid behind and came not with
the re‍ſt to the Valley of *Shinaar,* *Goropius* al-
‍ſo is cleerly of opinion ; who in like manner
a‍ſſerteth, that it is for certain, about *Ararat* fir‍ſt;
afterwards in the Plains of *Shinaar,* men after
the Deluge ‍ſeated them‍ſelves, and ‍ſtom either
of tho‍ſe places were di‍ſper‍ſed into ‍ſeveral parts
of the world. And if any ‍ſhall think the contrary, ‍ſaith he, that none remained behind, but all
went together to *Shinaar,* he will of great folly
accu‍ſe the ‍ſecond Parent of Mankind, that he
‍ſhould have ‍ſo little of the common ‍ſence of
men in him, as to make them all leave a‍ſſured
habitations, for uncertain dwellings ; ‍ſecure hou-
‍ſes, for open fields ; free ways, for encumbred
pa‍ſſages ; and known Meadows, for unknown
pa‍ſtures. By the ver‍ſes of *Sibylla* al‍ſo, which not
only *Jo‍ſephus,* but likewi‍ſe *Eu‍ſebius,* St. *Hierome,*
and others word for word remember, it ap-
pears that all came not together to *Shinaar.*

G. Bec. In-
do‍ſ. pag.
466.

Id, p. 132.

Πάντων ὁμοφώνων ὄντων ϖ͂ ἀνθρώπων πύργον ῳκοδέ-
μησαν τίνες ὑψηλότατον ὡς ὅτι ἔρανον ἀναβησόμενοι
δι' αὐτῶ. i. e. as *Goropius* renders the words,

Cum

Cum omnes homines ejusdem linguæ usum habe-rent, quidam eorum turrim ædificarunt altissimam, quasi per eam telum essent assensuri, when all men had the use of one same Tongue, *some of them built* a most high Tower, as if they had intended to have scaled Heaven thereby. When then *Sibylla,* as Sir *W. Raleigh* observes, making a limitation, saith, *some of them* [only some] built the Tower; and *Moses* witnesseth, that those that built it, came from the East into the West, it is plainly manifest, that all came not together with *Nimrod* unto *Shinaar,* but others remained behind in the Eastern parts. *All* therefore were not present at the building of the Tower, seeing that they went not *All* together; neither is it laid in Scripture that they did, which as it doth positively say, They were *All* of one speech; so it doth not definitively say, They *All* went.

Moreover, the exceeding multitude of People, wherein the East parts of the world first abounded; and wherein none of those by whom the Earth was planted after the *Confusion of Tongues,* are yet reported to have setled any Colonies, doth likewise very much convince, that the East Countries were peopled before the remove to *Babel.* For, that they were not left desolate upon this remove, but sufficiently provided both of Men and Citties, appeareth by *Heyl. Cosm.* those vast Armies of *Zoroaster* and *Staurobates;* *p. 7. & 831* of whom *Zoroaster* out of his own Kingdom of *Bactria,* brought into the field against *Ninus* the Monarch of *Assyria,* an Army of four hundred thousand fighting men; which manifesteth, saith *Heylin,* that *Bactria* was as soon peopled, as

as any Country since the general Deluge. For, it
could not have possibly been, that *Zoroaster* should
have raised so mighty an Army in the time of
Ninus, who was in succession but the third Monarch from *Nimrod*, had *Bactria* been planted,
but by a Colony sent out from *Shinaar*. The o-
ther *Staurobates* being King of *India* beyond
Indus, was invaded by *Semiramis* with an army
consisting of three Millions of footmen, one
million of horsemen, beside other mighty Forces
both for Land and Sea service ; whereof, saith
Sir *W. Raleigh*, if we believe but a third part, it
shall suffice to prove, that *India* was the first
Planted and Peopled Countrey after the Flood.
For *Staurobates* encountred her with an army
exceeding her numbers, *Staurobates avitis ma-*
joribus, quam quæ erant Semiramidis copiis, Stau-
robates drawing together of his own people
greater forces then those of *Semiramis* (saith *Di-*
odorus Siculus) defeated her.

Sir W. Ra,
hist. par. 1.
p. 99.

Now though considering the great Troops
that *Nimrod* might bring with him to *Babel*,
as by the building of the City and Tower may
appear, the numbers which *Semiramis* levied
might easily grow up, she being the Wife of *Ni-*
nus, the Son of *Belus*, who was the Son of *Nim-*
rod ; it was impossible nevertheless, that the
army of *Staurobates* should exceed hers, had his
numbers of *Indians* been encreased, but by Colonies sent into those parts, so late as the dispersion at *Babel* and *Confusion* of *Tongues*, unlesse
God had raised his Army out of Stones, or by
some such miracle. For, not any multiplication
natural (to use Sir *W. Raleigh's* own words)
could

could in such time produce so many bodies of Men, as were in the *Indian* Army victorious over *Semiramis*. When then *India* beyond *Indus* was in the time of *Staurobates* so fully peopled by those that remaining with *Noah* never came down to *Shinaar*; we need not doubt, but that they had then passed farther also; and as their numbers encreased, or desire of new seats invited them, made removes, and sent out Colonies to the more remote parts of *Asia*, till at length they setled in the remotest CHINA. Which Country that it was originally peopled by some of the posterity of *Noah* before the enterprise at *Babel*, *Heylin* conceives may probably be concluded. But of this hereafter. In the mean time, I might add for a farther evidence, that those that have written the actions of *Alexander* of *Macedon*, assure us, that he found more Cities and Sumptuosities in that little Kingdom of *Porus*, which lay side by side with the River *Indus*, than in all his other Travailes and Undertakings.

Heyl. Cosm. pag. 870.

Id. pa. 881.

But hereof we have as yet from *Heylin* somewhat more to say. He then in enumerating the old Inhabitants of *India*, relateth; that they were originally descended from the Sons of *Noah*, *before they left these Eastern parts, to go towards the unfortunate Valley of Shinaar*. We could not else have found this Country so full of people in the days of *Semiramis*, as that *Staurobates* to oppose her, could raise of natural *Indians* only, an army consisting of greater forces than that she led, and had compounded of several Nations to the number of four millions and upwards. A

matter

matter exceeding all credit, though neither
could make up a fourth part of that number, if
the *Indians* had been no other, than some one
of those Colonies, which were sent from *Babel*,
or rather a second or third swarme of those former Colonies, which went thence under the
command of the first Adventurers. For, that
any of the first Adventurers, who were present
at the building of the Tower of *Babel*, travailed
so far East, is not affirmed by any, who have laboured in the search of their Plantations. So
that I take it for a matter undeniable, that *the
Plantation of India preceded that of Babel*, though
by whom made, there is nothing to be said for
certain. Yet, saith he, if I might have liberty
to express my own conceptions, I am inclinable
to believe, that all the Eastern parts of *Persia*,
with CHINA, *and both the Indias, were peopled
by such of the Sons of* Sem, *as went not with the rest
to the Valley of Shinaar.* For, otherwise I can
see no reason, that the posterity of *Japhet*, should
plant the greatest part of the lesser *Asia*, and the
whole Continent of *Europe* with the Isles thereof, and that the Sons of *Cham* should spread
themselves over *Babylonia, Palæstine*, the three
Arabia's, and the whole Continent of *Africa*;
the posterity of *Sem* being shut up in a corner
of the greater *Asia*, hardly so big as some of the
Provinces taken up by the other Adventurers.
And therefore that an equal latitude may be allowed to the Sons of *Sem*, I think it not improbable to fix them in these Eastern Countries,
spreading themselves this way, as they grew in
numbers, *before the rest of the Adventurers went to*
seek.

seek out new fortunes at the Tower of Babel. Thus
far *Heylin.* Who hath set no less than four considerable remarks, as to our present enquiry
after the Plantations made before the dispersion at *Babel,* in this one and the same Para-
graph.

But here I meet with an objection, that *Atha-*
nasius Kircherus in his *China illustrata* asserts,
China was peopled by the posterity of *Cham,* after he came out of *Ægypt,* and therefore could
not be planted by any of the Sons of *Sem,* or
before the *Confusion at Babel.* In answer whereunto, I must take leave to give you *Kircherus*
his own words; by which you will find so slen-
der authority for his Assertion, that you will admire rather, how it was possible so learned a man
could ever fancy such a conceit. For, his principal, yea verily in manner his only argument is,
that because the *Ægyptians,* who were descended from *Cham,* used Hieroglyphicks; therefore
the *Chineses* did descend from *Cham,* because they
used Hieroglyphicks also. Whereby you may
observe, that if the *Mexicans* want their Ancestors, they may repair to *Kircherus,* and he will
presently inform them, that they came from
some of the posterity of *Cham* because they in
like manner as had the Ægyptians, have Hieroglyphicks in use. But why to confirm his opinion, did he not tell us, that the *Hebrews* were of
the seed of *Cham,* because they likewise as well
as the Ægyptians were circumcised? However
heare him, *Certe ut ad credendum inducar, magni*
momenti argumentum, sunt veteres isti sinensium
characteres Hieroglyphicorum in omnibus æmuli;
                                                Certain-

A. Kirch.
Ch. Ill. par.
6. pag. 226

Certainly, faith he, that I am induced to believe this, those ancient Characters of the *Chinoes* in all things imitating Hieroglyphicks, are an argument of great validity.

But Sir *W. Raleigh* will positively assure you, *Sir W. Ral.* that the *Chinoes* had Letters in use long before *hist. par. 1.* either the *Ægyptians* or *Phænicians*: *Semedo* will *pag. 98.* maintain, that they had the same Characters *A. Sem.* which they use at this day, and which were abstracted from those Hieroglyphicks, divers years *c. 6.* before *Kircherus* brings *Cham's* Plantation into *China*: *Vossius* can assert, that they have had the *Is. Voss. de* use of Letters longer by far than any people that *Ætat.* ever were: And *Martinius* makes appear ere *mun. p. 44.* long, that for Antiquity in the use of Letters, *M. Mart.* *China* excells all other parts of *Asia*; as also *Act. Sin. p. i* that *veteres isti Sinensium characteres Hieroglyphico-* *Id. Sin. His* *rum in omnibus æmuli*, were invented by the *Chinois* many ages before the flood. What is more to be said? *Kircherus* himself (allowing him his own computation) shall acknowledge *A. Kirch.* that *China* was both planted, and these their *Ch. Ill. par.* characters invented some Centuries of years *6. p. 225.* before the dispersion at *Babel*.

Now, though this is far more than sufficient to answer the objection, let us see nevertheless, how he conducts his Colony. He tells us then, *loco citato*, 'That *Cham* first out of *Ægypt* through ' *Persia*, and thence into *Bactria* conducted his ' Colonies, whom we conclude, faith he, to be ' the same with *Zoroaster* King of the *Bactrians*; ' but *Bactria* the farthest Region of *Persia*, is ' bounded by the Kingdom of the *Mogor*, or *In-* ' *dostan*, and thereby so opportunely scited, that

' they

' they might eafily from thence transferre their
' Colonies into *China*, the utmoft Nation of the
' habitable world, together alfo with the firft
' elements of Letters, which from their Father
' *Cham*, and *Mercurius Trefmegiftus* Counfellor of
' his Son *Mifraim*, and firft inventor of Hiero-
' glyphicks they had though rudely learned.
Now *Cham* cannot be faid to goe out of *Ægypt*
into *Bactria*, for after his arrival in *Ægypt*, he
never departed thence, but lived and died there
in the three hundred fifty fecond yeare after the

SirW.Ral. Deluge, as Sir *W. Raleigh* relates. *Heylin* hath
hift.par.1.p. told us lately, that *Bactria* was as foon peopled
197,198. as any Country fince the Univerfal Flood, o-
therwife it could not poffibly have oppofed
Ninus with fuch numbers as it did, if the fame
had been planted but by a Colony, fent out from
Shinaar; much lefs may we fay, if it were but
firft peopled from *Ægypt*, fo long time after.
For, Sir *W. Raleigh* finds *Cham* to have but begun his Kingdom there one hundred ninety one
years fucceeding the inundation of the world.
And as for *Mercurius Tres-Megiftus*, whom the
Greeks called *Hermes*, there were many of this
name, and how to diftinguifh them is difficult.
Two of them were famous in *Ægypt*, and there
worfhipped as Gods. The One (probably here
meant) was the fon of *Hylus*, whofe name faith
Bocc.lib.7. *Boccafe*, the *Ægyptians* feared to utter, as the
*pag.*126, *Jews* did their *Tetragrammaton*; the other was
127. the fon of this *Tref-Megiftus*, and for his wifdom
by his father called *Cath*; but which of thefe
two it was that taught the *Ægyptians* the ufe of
Letters, Writers much differ; and no lefs alfo
about

about the Age in which they lived. For *Iſaack-ſon* and others, place them about the time that *Abraham* was called out of *Haran* or *Charran* in-to the land of *Canaan*; others ſuppoſe the firſt and moſt ancient to have been *Joſeph* the ſon of *Jacob*; others again, that he was *Moſes* himſelf; and Sir *W. Rawleigh* with ſome Hiſtorians find them not to have flouriſhed until the days of *Moſes*; when as the *Chinois* had enjoyed their *now* letters at leaſt five hundred years before.

It was *Sem* that inhabited the Countrey of *A-ſia* beginning at *Euphrates*, and extending to the *Indian* Ocean ſea, ſaith *Joſephus* : To the poſte-rity of *Sem* befel the parts of *Aſia* from *Indæa* Eaſtward, ſaith *Purchas*; the Eaſtern parts of *A-ſia*, together with ſome of the Southern, were peopled by the generations of *Sem*; ſaith *G. J. Voſſius.* And with theſe *Raleigh, Heylin,* and *Ayn-ſworth* agree, as you have heard. Whereas *Cham* and his off-ſpring poſſeſſed the South of *Aſia* and *Africa*, as the ſame Authors aſſert.

Joſep. Ant. Jud. lib.1. cap.7. Purch. Pil-grimage, lib.1.p. 37. G.J.Voſ. Chron Sac. pa.52. Aynſwor. in Gen.10.

Neither could *Cham* be *Zoroaſter*, it is a fancy, ſaith Sir *W. Raleigh*, of little probability. For *Cham* was the paternal Anceſtor of *Ninus*, the father of *Chus*, the grandfather of *Nimrod*, whoſe ſon was *Belus*, the father of *Ninus*, which *Ninus* ſlew *Zoroaſter* in *Bactria*, as Hiſtoriographers una-nimouſly accord. Wherefore, and for that *Cham* never removed out of *Ægypt* after his ſettlement there, into *Bactria*; *Cham* could not be *Zoroaſter* King of the *Bactrians*, nor from thence ever tranſ-ferr Colonies into *China*, as *Kircherus* would per-ſwade. But in all probability, *China* was after the Flood firſt planted either by *Noah* himſelf, or

Sir W. Ral. hiſt. par.1. p.169.

ſome

some of the sons of *Sem*, before the remove to
Shinaar. For, such Principles of Theology, as
amongst the *Chinois*, we shall shortly hear of,
could not proceed from the wicked and idola-
trous race of accursed *Cham*, but from those only
that were, *de civitate Dei*, of the City of God.

The most remote parts then of the Eastern
World, being planted before the dispersion at
Babel, and until the *Confusion* of *Tongues*, the
whole Earth being of *one language and one lipp*,
it must indisputably succeed, that *Noah* and whosoever remained with him, which came not with
the rest to the valley of *Shinaar*, and consequently
by their absence thence, had no hand in that vain
attempt, could not be concerned in the *Confusion*
there, nor come within the curse of *confounded
Languages*; but retained the PRIMITIVE
Tongue, as having received it from *Noah*, and
likewise carry the same with them to their several Plantations, in what part of the East soever
they setled themselves, aswel as *Nimrod* and his
Troops brought it with them to *Shinaar*. And
hence it is, that *Goropius* saith, Because the *Cimme-
rians* were not at the *Confusion* of *Babel*, therefore there is no question to be made, but that their
Language was the PRIMITIVE.

Hence the same Author, Because those that
were left behind to plant *Margiana*, were not at
the building of the Tower, it must be necessarily
acknowledged, in regard the Language was not
confined to any, but general to all, aswel unto
those at *Shinaar*, as all people elsewhere, that the
ANCIENT Language, which before the
Confusion was common to the universal World,
remained

*G. Becd.
Indos. pag.
534.*

Id. pag. 533

remained with thofe of *Margiana.* Hence Sir *W.* *Sir W. Ral. Hiftor. par. 1. pag.* 158. *Raleigh*, it is conjectured , that thofe of the race of *Sem* which came into *Chaldæa*, were of *Nimrod's* Troop, and removed with him thither: yet, in regard they were no partners in the unbelieving work of the Tower, therefore they did retain the firft and moft antient Language , which the firft Age had left to *Noah* , and *Noah* to *Sem* and his Iffues Hence *Heylin* alfo, That fome Plan- *Heyl. Cof. p. 7.* tations had no reference to the *Confufion* of *Tongues*, being made before it, on the fending out of fuch Colonies, as were neateft to the place, where the Ark did reft. But how general foever the confent is, what needeth prophane teftimony; when facred Hiftory plainly teacheth us, That the Language of *Thofe* only that were at *Babel* was confounded, and not of *Thofe* that were abfent thence, and not guilty of that mif-believing work. The words of the holy Penman, *Gen.* 11. *v.* 5, 6, 7, 8. are. *And the Lord came down to fee the City, and the Tower, which the Children of men build-ed. And the Lord faid, Behold, the people is one, and they have all one Language, and this they begin to do; and now nothing will be reftrained from them, which they have imagined to do. Go to, let us go down, and* THERE *confound* THEIR *Language, that* THEY *may not underftand one anothers Speech. So the Lord fcattered* THEM *abroad from* THENCE *upon the face of all the Earth, and they left off to build the City.*

Which can admit no other conftruction , than that the Language of *Thofe*, that were THERE, that is, at that place in *Babylonia*, not in *India* or elfewhere was confounded. So in like manner

D   THEIR

THEIR Language, *i. e. Their* Language that
were with *Nimrod*, and of this Western Colony;
not the Language of *Noah*, and his Plantations
in the East. Again also, That THEY, to wit,
those *children of men,* that built the Tower; not
those generations that had no hand in building
of the same, might *not understand one anothers
speech.*

Furthermore, the Lord scattered THEM

Sir W. Ral. abroad from THENCE, " Which, saith Sir
par. 1. pag. " W. *Raleigh,* hath no other sence, but that the
104. " Lord scattered THEM, *viz.* those that built
" this Tower, for those were from THENCE
(to wit, *Babel*) " dispersed into all the Regions
" of the North and South, and to the Westward.
" The East being inhabited before.

But let us consider the Context. The Scene
was the valley of *Shinaar*; *They found a plain in
the land of Shinaar, and they dwelt there.* v. 2. The
Offenders were *Nimrod* and his Troops; *And
they said, Go to, let us build us a City and a Tower,
whose top may reach unto Heaven, and let us make us
a name, lest we be scattered abroad upon the face of
the whole Earth.* ver. 4. The fear of a Judgment
brought a Judgment upon them. And as the Offenders were those only at *Shinaar,* so the Language of those only at *Shinaar* was confounded.
Go to, let us go down (saith the Lord) *and there
confound their Language, that they may not understand one anothers speech.* v. 7 The punishment being justly inflicted, where only the offence lay,
and upon those solely that had offended. No man
shall answer for anothers fault: it is both the Law
and Gospel. *The soul that sinneth, it shall die,*
Ezech.

Ezech. 18. v. 20. *For we muſt all appear before the judgment ſeat of Chriſt, that every one may receive the things done in his body, according to that he hath done, whether it be good or bad;* 2 Corinth. cap. 5. v. 10. And I muſt not omit that the marginal notes of our *Bible,* for the more clear expoſition of the Text we are upon, refer us to the *Wiſedome* of *Solomon,* cap. 10. v. 5. where it is written; *Moreover, the Nations in their wicked conſpiracy being confounded, Shee* [Wiſedome] *found out the righteous, and preſerved him blameleſs unto God, and kept him ſtrong againſt the tender compaſſion of his ſon.* Whereby, though it may be conceived, that in the particular, this alludes unto *Abraham* his ſacrificing of *Iſaac;* yet in the general, it is moſt evident, moſt certain thereby, that *Thoſe* only that had offended in the conſpiracy of the building of the Tower, had their Language confounded; and were convicted by that Judgment.

Thus from Scripture and approved Hiſtory hath been made appear, That the Ark reſted in the Eaſt; That *Noah* planted not far from the place, where it took ground; and from thence by himſelf, and his off-ſpring, that abode with him, peopled the Eaſtern parts of the World, together with *China;* and that theſe Plantations were undertaken and ſetled before the remove to *Shinaar,* and *Confuſion* of Tongues, by thoſe that never came at *Babel;* and could not therefore be ingaged in that preſumptuous work. But who they were of his off-ſpring that *Noah* kept with him, whether of the ſons of *Joctan;* or of all the reſt a certain number (*Cham* and his iſſue only excepted)

Sir W. Ral-
Hiſt par. I.
pag. 101.
ted)cannot, ſaith Sir W. Raleigh, be known: Nevertheleſs we are not to doubt; but that their numbers were ſo great, as not only ſufficed to huſ-
band thoſe Plantations that Noah had ſetled, but
alſo to ſend forth Colonies elſewhere, as occaſion
required.

The Scripture alſo plainly declareth, That the
curſe of *Confounded Languages* fell upon thoſe only
that were preſent upon the place at Babel, and
perſonally acted in that ungodly deſign there.
And therefore we may warrantably conclude,
That either the PRIMITIVE Language is
to be found amongſt thoſe Plantations that were
made before the *Babylonian* Enterpriſe, by thoſe
that were abſent thence, and had not offended
therein; or elſe it cannot be appropriated to any
Nation now extant in the World, or at this day
known. For, as the people at Babel, that had
ſolely offended, were therefore from Shinaar
ſcattered throughout all the other parts of the
un-inhabited Earth; ſo only the Language which
they brought with them thither, was there for
their offence confounded; and, as is conceived,
divided into ſeveral other Languages, paſſing at
this day amongſt us by the name of MOTHER-
Tongues, which that they were ſeventy two in
number, he that hath a mind to pleaſe himſelf
with believing it, ſhall not diſpleaſe me.

Heyl. Coſm.
pag. 17.
Now here, *Heylin* is ſo courteous, as to befriend
me with an Objection. That admitting it for
granted, that thoſe who ſtaid behind with Noah,
ſpake the ſame Language which was common to
the Fathers before the Flood (be it the *Hebrew* or
what elſe ſoever it was) there ſeems no reaſon to
the

the contrary, but that it might in time be branched into feveral Languages or Dialects of the
fame one Language, by the Commerce and En-
tercourfe which they had with Nations of a different fpeech. To which, is thus anfwered, That
not only Commerce and Intercourfe, but alfo
Time and Conqueft may poffibly caufe the alteration of a Language, yet in regard that Conquefts are of divers kinds, and Intercourfe and
Commerce of different natures, fuch alteration
cannot be effected by every manner of Commerce
and Conquefts.

For, on the one fide, where an Invader enters
a Country with a refolution wholly to difpoffefs
and expel the Natives, it inevitably follows, that
the fpeech of that Country, muft, being fubdued,
receive fuch an abfolute change, as that no other,
than that which the Conqueror brings with him
can remain; And thus we find, it fucceeded at the
conqueft of the Land of *Canaan* by the *Ifraelites*;
who generally, expelling the *Canaanites*, introduced their own Language (whatever it were) and
extirpated the former. Where alfo an Invader
hath made fuch a full Conqueft, as that he can
clear, or (as I may fay) drive the Countrey, and
carry away the whole body of the Natives into
captivity, there, no doubt is to be made, but that
the Language of the vanquifhed muft undergo a
manifeft alteration. And thus we find that in fo
fhort a time as the captivity of *Babylon*, thofe of
Judah had in fuch manner loft their fpeech, as
at their return home, they could not underftand
the Book of their own Laws, but by an Interpreter. *Nehem. cap. 8. v. 7. 8.*

But

But on the other fide, where the Invader enters, to poffefs new dwellings, and plant himfelf and people; when he neither carries the Natives elfewhere into captivity, nor utterly expels them, the old Language of that Countrey çannot be extirpated; but may be altered, and by the mixture with new commers after long tract of time, become generally a new kind of fpeech. Thus the invafions of the *Huns, Goths,* and *Longobards,* and their Conquefts, brought a new Language into *Italy.* And thus the *Goths* and *Vandals, Saracens* and *Moors* into *Spain.* So likewife where a forein Enemy, out of an ambitious defire of Fame and Glory, and for eternizing his name invades a Countrey, and having obtained a victory, upon a certain tribute condefcended unto by the Natives, for acknowledgment of fubjection, acquitteth it again, there it is impoffible, the fpeech of that Countrey fhould be changed. For, it cannot be imagined, that the Kingdom of *Porus,* into which *Alexander* the *Great* no fooner leaped, than leaped out of it again, could by fuch a conqueft, have the Language thereof, either altered or corrupted. In like manner, the conquefts of the *French* in *Italy,* no more altered the *Italian* Tongue, than our Invafions of *Scotland,* did the *Pictifh,* or *Scottifh* fpeech.

There is moreover another kind of Conqueft, where the Victor takes up the Manners and Cuftomes of the vanquifhed, and tranfporteth into his own Country the Language, Arts, and Sciences of thofe that he hath overcome. For the *Romans* together with their victory over *Greece,* brought home with them, Sculpture, Painting, and the
Language

Language of that People alſo ; which *Plutarch* in the life of *M. Cato* telleth us, moſt of the *Romans* ſtudied. Yet we find not, that the *Latine* Tongue was corrupted, but rather refined thereby ; and if it were refined, then it was altered, for every refining is changing. But, this ſome will perhaps ſay, is directly contrary to what is objected : for, here in this caſe, not the Language of the vanquiſhed by the Conqueror, but the Language of the Conqueror by the vanquiſhed comes to receive an alteration. After the ſame manner, by their conqueſts in *Aſia,* the *Romans* learned luxury and riot, to wear ſilk, and live effeminately ; the *Aſiatiques* in the mean time compoſing themſelves to the antient temperance, frugality and diſcipline of their Lords and Maſters the *Romans.* Thus alſo we find, that the *Macedonians* long before, when they had conquered *Perſia,* became not only in Language and Attire, but alſo in Diſcipline and Cuſtomes *Perſians* rather, than the *Perſians, Macedonians.* And this oftentimes happeneth, as all Hiſtory informs, where the Conqueror is either barbarous, or not in ſuch a degree civilized, as thoſe that are ſubdued by him, Or elſe efflated by ſucceſs, wholly gives himſelf over to licentiouſneſs, diſdaining the manners of his native Countrey.

As for *Time,* it may, having eſpecially Commerce its attendant, prevail ſomewhat herein; For, we our ſelves can ſcarcely now underſtand the Language that was uſed in the days of *Chaucer.* And yet nevertheleſs we know, that the *Latine* Tongue, hath from *Cæſars* time, maugre all conqueſts and intercourſe whatſoever, received

not

not the least alteration, but remaineth both in the Characters and reading the same, as then, and is as generally, if not better understood, in these days, than it was fifteen hundred years since.

Lastly, concerning *Intercourse* and *Commerce*, it is true, that in such a Nation, where a general Commerce is permitted, and free access granted to all Strangers to trade and inhabit; aswel in the Inland parts of the Countrey, as upon the Frontires or Sea-coasts; there a change of Language may by degrees happen. And we need not go far for Example. For, with us our selves, by this means chiefly, the *Saxon* Tongue, since the time of the *Normans* is utterly lost. Insomuch that what by *Latinizing*, *Italianizing*, *Frenchizing*, and [as we must have it called forsooth,] *Refinizing*, or rather *Non-sencizing*, our old Language is so corrupted and changed, that we are so far from *Saxonizing*, as we have scarcely one significant word of our MOTHER speech left.

But on the contrary, where *Commerce* is made, and *Intercourse* allowed, upon the Seacoasts and Frontires only, there we find the Language of the Natives in the In-land parts, to remain without suffering any alteration. Hence *Cæsar* telleth us, that he found some footsteps of the *Gaulish* Language upon the coast of *Britain*, when within the land (though he advanced not far) the *British* Tongue was spoken purely. And hence in *Ise-and*, though about four hundred years since conquered by the *Norvegians*, in regard there is little access of strangers, but only as some part of the Maritime shores affordeth; as also because they

they suffer not their unexperienced youth to travail abroad into other Countries, the old *Runique*
or *Gothique* Tongue in manner yet continueth,
and is by divers of the Inhabitants understood,
when in all the Septentrional World besides, it is
utterly forgotten and extinct. But what shall we
say of the *Basquish* or antient Language of *Spain*?
which notwithstanding all the Invasions of the
Carthaginians, *Romans*, *Goths*, *Vandals*, *Moors* remaineth yet pure in *Biscay*, whatever *Commerce*
and Intercourse soever that Countrey hath in all
times enjoyed. Insomuch that the Inhabitants
upon one side of the River running from the
mountains of *Ordunia* to *Bilboa*, and which carries the Iron-mills, speaking the MOTHER
Language, understand not one word, unless by
an Interpreter, what those on the other side of
the same River say. What of the *Irish* Tongue?
which Countrey, although we have kept under
subjection by lawful conquest, near five hundred
years, setled many Plantations therein, and permitted continually free *Commerce*; yet nevertheless the natural Language of the Countrey continueth throughout most parts of that Kingdom
pure and untainted at this day. And which is remarkable, if a child born of *English* Parents there,
and as curiously overseen as possibly a child can
be from hearing of the Native *Irish* speak, chance
to hear but one word of that Language, he will
sooner remember the same, and be apter to repeat it again, than he shall any one word of *English*, though twenty times spoken before him.
What of the old *British* Tongue? since that
through all the conquests of the *Romans*, *Saxons*,
Danes,

Danes, and *Normans*, and after unlimited conversation with most Nations of the World, it hath passed currant, and is yet remaining in *Wales*. In like manner, the *Arabique* continueth incorrupt in the hilly parts of *Granata* : and the antient *Epirotique* in the high, wooddy, and more mountanous parts of *Epirus*.

By all which it appeareth, That not any kind of *Conquest* can wholly alter or extirpate the natural Language of a people, except by generally expelling the Natives, or transplanting them elsewhere. And that *Commerce* and *Intercourse* where a mixture of several Nations is wholly permitted, may in long tract of *Time* produce an absolute alteration; but where tolerated on the Sea-coasts or confines of a Country only, can neither alter a Language, nor branch it into several Dialects of the same, but may possibly in those places corrupt it, whilst the Inland parts nevertheless enjoy purely their MOTHER Tongue.

When then it is reputed ridiculous to hear that *Adam* spake *Dutch* in Paradice : And when we consider, that the *Hebrews* have no surer foundation to erect their Language upon, than only a bare Tradition of their own, which we all know is so infamous an *Historian*, as Wisemen neither report after it, nor give credit to any thing they receive from it : As also that the *Samaritans* by their often removes were but a mungrel people, and in regard of their continual commerce with Nations of a different speech; and the many storms and tempests of Wars and Conquests, which they were always subject to, have but a mungrel Language; for though it hath, as is not

to

to be denied, some proper and peculiar words of
its own, neverthelefs it oftentimes ufeth the *Arabique*, and in forming of Nouns and Verbs, sometimes follows the *Hebrew*, sometimes the *Chaldæan*,
wherewith it is of great affinity. And though
they may have had, as they pretend, the *Pentateuch*
of *Mofes* written in a ftrange Character, the
Samaritan, as they call it, yet their having had it in
their cuftody contributes not an *Iota* to the Antiquity of their fpeech, or that it fhould have anci̇ent-
ly been the PRIMITIVE Tongue, in regard thofe
Characters not much differ from the modern *He-
braique*, unlefs where either by the negligence of
the Scribe, or variety of the Copies, fome diverfity appears; as our famous Doctor *Brian Walton*,
late Bifhop of *Chefter* in his Introduction to the
reading of the Oriental Tongues hath very learnedly obferved : And when in like manner we
confider, that it cannot with any probability of
Truth be refolved, that the *Phænicians*, who are
generally fuppofed to be the wicked off-fpring of
accurfed *Cham*, the principal Actors, and Often-
dors in that daring confpiracy at *Babel*, fhould
enjoy fo great a priviledge, as to carry away with
them, and be infranchifed to that Sacred Language, which even in the time of innocency was
fpoken between God and Man : Why may we
not reflect upon the CHINOIS ? For we fhall
make appear, that *They* were primitively planted in CHINA, if not by *Noah* himfelf, by fome
of the Iffue of *Sem*, before the remove of *Nimrod*
to *Shinaar*, and the *Confufion* of *Tongues* at *Babel*;
Their Language to be the felf fame at this day, as
when they were firft planted and began to be a
people;

*B. Walt,
Intr. ad
Ling. Or,
p. 18, 19,*

people; Their Country never subject to any such conquest, as could prejudice, but rather dilate their language ; *Their* Laws in all times to have prohibited forein *Commerce* and *Intercourse* ; and *Their* dominions ever shut up against strangers, never permitting any to set footing within *Their* Empire, unless by way of Embassy solely ; nor suffering *Their* own Natives to travail abroad without especial licence from their Emperour: So jealous have they evermore been, lest *Their* Language and Customes should be corrupted. Considering which, together with their infinite multitudes of People, and perpetual flourishing in Peace, and all Arts and Sciences, whilst every Nation almost throughout the whole Universe besides, have more than once in time been over-run and conquered; it may with much probability be asserted, *That the Language of the Empire of CHIN A, is, the PRIMITIVE Tongue, which was common to the whole World before the Flood* ; and that it could never be branched into several Languages, or *Dialects* of the same one Language, by the *Commerce* and *Intercourse* which they had with Nations of a different speech; when they never had *Commerce* or *Intercourse* with any, Nor were ever known to these parts of the World (scarcely to their adjoyning Neighbours) till about an hundred and fifty years since, by the *Portugals* and *Spaniards* they were discovered.

But I find St. *Hierome*, and others that follow him, object, That the *Hebrew* was the PRIMITIVE Language, in regard that all the proper names of men before the Deluge, and immediately
ately

ately after the same appear to be naturally *He-brew*. And that it was necessary the Sacred Scripture should be delivered in that Language, which *Adam* and the rest used before the Flood. To which the answer is obvious, that the Names might be first imposed in the PRIMITIVE Language, and that it was an easie matter for the succeeding Ages, understanding by Tradition what they meant, to transferr them into the *He-brew* Tongue; whereby also the Names of men might equally answer to the Names of places, which otherwise they could not do; for throughout the whole course of the Books of *Moses* and *Joshuah* it is manifest, that the names of the Places and Cities of *Canaan*, the antient names, I mean, by which they were called before ever the *Israelites* came to dwell in them, were *Hebrew* names. Neither was there any more necessity, that the sacred Oracles of God should be written in the first and most perfect speech, than for CHRIST to be born of the most honorable and richest Parents, and live in the most splendid and delicious manner. For, that the World might know, man is not to attribute any thing to his own merits or greatness, but that God giveth all his *Grace gratis*, he hath ever chosen humble and lowly Ministers of his *Grace*. Thus of *Abraham* the son of an Idolater, and maker of Idols, he made choice, to be the first founder of Circumcision. And so ordained, that CHRIST himself, when he was to be born should scarcely have a roof to shelter him, when he newly came out of his Mothers womb, from the inclemency of the Air. And when CHRIST came to redeem us from

sin

sin and death, he elected not those, to preach his Gospel throughout the World, that were of the Schools of the Philosophers, or of *Demosthenes* or *Cicero*, but made choice of rude men, of a rude manner of life, Fishermen, and Boatmen to be the Heralds for proclaiming of his Victory. Neither was it any King or Monarch, but an *Abject*, who was cast forth and exposed to the mercy of cruel waves, and cruelty of merciless Crocodiles, that delivered the *Israelites* from their slavery in *Ægypt*. And if we run throughout all, throughout all we shall find, those to have pleased God most, that are wont to displease men most. There is no reason therefore any should think that so contrary to the doctrine of God, either the *Typical Law* or the *fulfilling of the Law* should be given in that Language which all others excelled. But, as the *fulfilling of the Law*, which relateth chiefly to the *Gentiles*, was written in the *Greek* Tongue; because that Language being, as it were, then generally known, the Nations might by reading it, the sooner be converted, and brought within the sheepfold of CHRIST. So no doubt, the *Typical Law*, wherein the Church of the *Israelites* was solely concerned, was written, not in the PRIMITIVE, but for their better instruction, in the old *Hebrew* Tongue, which *Abraham* brought, not out of *Chaldæa*, but learned in the land of *Canaan*, whereby it became the Language of his Posterity, and by them was vulgarly spoken, until, as some will have it, their Captivity. And this the Scripture doth in direct terms testifie; when upon the calling of the *Ægyptians* it is said. *In that day shall five Cities in the land of Ægypt*

speak.

speak the language of Canaan, and swear to the LORD of Hosts. Isai. 19. v. 18. By which we are taught, that the *Ægyptians* should not only be brought to offer the same sacrifices and oblations to the LORD, as the *Israelites* did, but speak the same speech with them also, which was the Language of the land of *Canaan.* From whence we will at present depart, to enter upon our travail into CHINA.

MARTINUS Martinius in his famous *Chinique Atlas,* after his much celebrating of *Asia* in general, for having been the place of our first Parents, and Paradise, and original of all things, proceedeth to the Antiquities of the Empire of CHINA, in particular, after this manner. But of *Asia* it self, saith he, there is no part (at least since the universal Deluge) more Noble, more Antient, or more fertile than this extreme part thereof, whether Politique Government, the use of Letters, or Industry be respected. For, the History of it by the *Chinois* themselves even from all Antiquity written, comprehendeth almost three thousand years before the birth of CHRIST, as more evidently by the Epitomy and Chronology collected out of their Annals appears. Ever since which time they are said to have had Letters, Moral Philosophy, and Mathematical Sciences especially; which both their more than Antique observations of the Stars, and those Laws of Government written in most antiently antient Volumes; and at these very times extant, more than sufficiently shew and declare. In the Epistle Dedicatory of his *Atlas* he premiseth thus, In these Mapps, I present unto your view the

M. Marti. Atl. Sin. pag. 1.

the scituation and limits of the most vast Empire of the *Chinois*, equal almost unto all *Europe*. It hath ever since the Flood of *Noah*, been inhabited by a most industrious and civil people, but hitherto wholly inaccessable to Strangers, until now at last for the salvation of Souls, after great trouble and anxiety those of my Society, saith he, have gained entrance thereinto.

If. Voss. de Ætat. Mun. pag. 44. *Isaacus Vossius* (of whom our famous Dr. *Usher* late Archbishop of *Armagh*, gives so clear a testimony, that we are obliged to acknowledge him a most learned man) in his dissertation of the true Age of the world, having discoursed of those Nations, that are the greatest pretenders to Antiquity, as the *Hebrews*, *Samaritans*, *Chaldeans* and *Ægyptians*, brings up the *Chinois* in the rear, and of them delivers his testimony, after these words. Let us now come to those, that not so much by their own, as the name of their neighbours are called *Chinois*. I mean, saith he, the *Serians*. A race of men by far the most skilled in letters of all the people that ever were. They preserve a continued History compiled from their monuments, and annual exploits of four thousand five hundred yeares. Writers they have more antient than even *Moses* himself. Ever since their beginning to be a Nation, they have never been corrupted by intercourse with strangers, nor ever known what wars and contentions meant; but addicted only to quietness, delight, and contemplation of Nature, have run through the space (*plusquam*) of *more than four thousand years*, unknown indeed to other Nations, but enjoying to themselves their own felicity at pleasure.   Now,

Now, in regard *Voſſius* names them *Serians,* I *M. Mart. Atl. Sin. pag.16.* am compelled before proceeding farther to certifie, that this outmoſt Region of the known World, which *Martinius* calls the extreme part of *Aſia,* is by ſome called *Serica, Sina,* or *China* by others, by the *Tartars Cathay* and *Mangin,* and which every man wonders at, not any of all theſe names, is at all known unto the *Chinois* themſelves, that of *Mangin* excepted, the *Tartars* having ironically in deriſion put that upon them, as ſcoffing at their being over arrogant and proud of their civilities ; for *Mangin* in the *Tartarian* Tongue ſignifies barbarous people. But the *Chinois* call their Empire *Chunghoa,* and *Chunghue,* either name, ſaith *Martinius,* being impoſed for the excellency thereof. *This* expreſſing the middle Kingdome (they ſuppoſing themſelves to be ſcited in the middle of the World) *That* ſignifies the middle Garden or Flower rather. But how much theſe myſterious reaſons of Names may import their Language to be the PRIMITIVE Tongue, I ſhall leave unto *Martinius, Goropius,* and others, ere our diſcourſe brings us to a period, to acquaint you.

But ſeeing *Martinius* referred us to his Epito- *M. Mart. Sin. Hiſt. lib.1. p.12.* my of the Hiſtory of *China,* we are not to neglect him therein. *Illud pro certo compertum, Sinemſem de diluvio Hiſtoriam non multum à Noetico abeſſe, quippe quæ ter mille circiter annis vulgarem Chriſti Epocham prægreditur.* It is for certain, ſaith he, That the *Chinique* Hiſtory that mentioneth the Deluge reacheth not far from the Flood of *Noah,* for it precedeth the birth of CHRIST accor-

E ding

ding to the vulgar computation about three
thousand years.

Now, for that we are to make great use of
Martinius his Authority, I conceive it not impertinent to let you know, that he professeth, after
his having lived many years amongst the *Chinois*,
to have with great care and long study epitomiz-
ed their History from their Original Annals,
and innumerable their other Books, yet extant
even at this day amongst them from their first
beginning to be a Nation. And to have brought
it down with all clearness and integrity to the
incarnation of CHRIST, and since, to these
times also; though that part thereof, we are
not so happy, as to have yet made publique.

M. Mart.
Sin. Hist.
Epist. ad
Lect.
In this their History from the time of the
Flood, he very much enclineth to repose an assured confidence, telling us in his Epistle to the
Reader, That the fidelity thereof is so much the
more warrantable, as that the *Chinois* for themselves only writ the same; either contemning or
not knowing forein Nations; so that, seeing they
neither regarded to please Strangers, nor boast
of their own actions, they had no occasion to deliver untruths or report Fables. So much the less
because they have no Nobility either for Antiquity of birth or time to flatter. Every the poorest
man amongst them, if deserving it by his learning, being capable of the highest preferment.
Hence it proceeds, saith he, that about their History there are no controversies or disputes with
them, no difference in the succession of their Emperors, nor genealogies of their Royal families,

of

of which nevertheleſs amongſt us ſo little care
is taken, that every Chronologer almoſt differeth
from another.

Now, though *Martinius* hath this opinion of ⟨*id. p. 124*⟩
the ſincerity of their Annals ſince the time of the
Flood ; yet as to the Age preceding the ſame, the
Chinois themſelves give little or no credit to
what is related in them , during their Government by the heads of Families, but from the time
they began to be ruled by a Monarch , of which,
opportunity ſerving, we ſhall take farther notice,
and at preſent adviſe you only. That whereas by
their Hiſtory it appears *Fotrius* who was their
firſt Monarch began his reign over them, about
three thouſand years before the birth of
C H R I S T, after the common Chronology,
Martinius tells us, that the credit thereof muſt
reſt at their own doors, for a matter of ſuch mo-
ment he will not take upon him to decide ; in
regard it conſents not with the judgment of our
Chronologers, that aſſign a much leſs ſpace of
time from the Flood of *Noah.* Yet nevertheleſs, ⟨*M. Mart.*⟩
ſaith he, the opinion of the *Chinois* ſeems not on ⟨*Sin. Hiſt.*⟩
every ſide to be rejected : Several of the Chro- ⟨*lib. 1. p. 134*⟩
nologers of *Europe* favour it ; the *Seventy Inter-*
preters make for it, ſo alſo *Samoſatenus* and others,
neither doth the *Roman* Martyrologe, or computation of the *Greeks* much diſſent there-
from.

But hearken unto *Voſſius* (*Martinius* conſenting ⟨*Jſ. Voſ. de*⟩
with him) *Miranda artis & naturæ opera quæ ex hu-* ⟨*Ætat. Mun.*⟩
jus regni cognitione ad nos perlata ſunt, non eſt hujus ⟨*p. 48. 4-*⟩
loci recenſere. Ea ſaltem referemus quæ de annis & ⟨*M. Mart.*⟩ ⟨*Ail. Sin.*⟩
antiquitate gentis comperimus, Serum itaque tem- ⟨*pag. 164*⟩

E 2

pus historicum incipit annis ante natum Christum
2847. The wonderful works both of Nature
and Art, which, faith he, by the discovery of this
Empire, are arrived at our knowledge, this is no
place to mention. We shall relate at least what
we find of the Age and Antiquity of the Nation.
The Historical time therefore of the *Serians* begins two thousand and eight hundred forty seven
years before CHRIST was born. This said,
and having afterwards computed from the said
time, the several reigns of their Emperors according to their several families, he thus concludes, *A*
principio itaque regni Serum, usque ad finem præsen-
tis anni, qui est 1658 post Christum natum, colliguntur
*in universum anni 4505.*From the beginning ther-
fore of the *Serian* Empire unto the end of this present year one thousand six hundred fifty eight after
the birth of CHRIST, are numbred in the to-
tal four thousand five hundred five years. Whereby
appears, that according to the vulgar *Æra*,
which *Martinius* follows, and which makes from
the Creation to the Flood of *Noah* one thousand
six hundred fifty six years; and from thence to
the coming of CHRIST into the World two
thousand two hundred ninety four years ; the
Historical time of the *Chineis* begins several A-
ges, to wit, five hundred fifty three years before
the Universal Deluge, computing to the year one
thousand six hundred fifty eight : as *Vossius*
doth.

Al. Sem.
Rel. del.
Cin. par.1.
cap.22.
Alvarez Semedo, a diligent Author for his time,
as writing his relation of *China* about thirty years
since ; discoursing of the first Emperours thereof, wholly omits *Fotrius,* with his five Successors

till

till *Jaus*, the better to difpenfe with their Chronology before the Flood, of which he feems to have no great opinion : the moft favorable judgment he will allow thereof, being that their Emperor *Jaus* might precede that deftruction twelve years. And though he faith, there may be a mif-computation thereby in the Hiftory of this Emperour, and his Succeffors *Xunus*, and *Tnus* ; he doth neverthelefs affure us, that the matters related of them, are very coherent with their Succeffions. His words being ; *Ad ogni modo, benche via fia errore nel tempo, dall' hiftoria di quefto Imperatore e feguenti ; è certo che le cofe vanno coherenti con le loro fucceffioni.* He tells us alfo, that thefe three Emperors are by the *Chinois* reputed Saints, of whom they relate many things, and that certainly there is no doubt to be made, but that they were great Philofophers ; and much enclined to moral vertue.

But in regard *Martinius* in his *Tartarian* War premifeth, that he hath in his *Atlas* of *China* deduced and taken their Hiftory from their own antient Records ever fince the time of *Noah*. We therefore beginning alfo at the Deluge, will now return to their Antiquity.

Of the Deluge their Writers make much mention, but of the original and caufe thereof, as can yet be found, they give not any account. Which therefore whether it were that of *Noah*, or fome other peculiar to the *Chinois*, as the *Ogygian* antiently in *Attica*, or the *Deucalionian* in *Theffaly* appears not. For which a manifeft reafon may be given, becaufe they have always reputed themfelves to be the only great people of

the

the World; and that it contained either few or
no other Nations besides themselves; and those
generally so contemptible, as that they held them
scarcely worthy the conquering; much less en-
quiring after what successes or calamities befel
them. And therefore with our Authors, I am
very much resolved to believe, that, that flood
which happened in *China* in the time of *Jaus*
their seventh Empeeror, was the universal flood.
For our Chronologers of *Europe* referr the flood
of *Noah* to the very reign of this Emperor, and
the *Chinois* themselves in their Annals relate,
that during his government great numbers of
People flocked into their Countrey; and that at
the same time it was drowned, and overflown
with waters, which were brought in by the Deluge, *Eas Author Sinicus ait diluvio invectas,* saith
Martinius in the life of *Jaus.* Considering which
together with the coherence of Time, this Deluge that thus drowned *China* could certainly be
no other, than that, that drowned the whole
World besides. And the flocking in of those people thither in such numbers, seemeth much to
confirm the same. For thereby is evidently difcovered as wel the great fears, that generally at
last, possessed all Nations, as the hopes they had
by their flying out of the low and champain Regions adjoyning, to avoid and escape the threat-
ning danger, upon the great and high mountains,
that run throughout, and as it were surround
the *Chinique* World.

M. Mart.   But let us see how our Author proceedeth.
Sin. Hist.   And because that under this Emperor mention
Lib.1.p.39. is made of the gathering together of waters,
                                              which

which the History of *China* calleth the Deluge;
and, that the *European* Chronologers from more
certain grounds (from the computation of *Mo-*
ses he might as wel have said) reduce the flood of
Noah to the time of this Emperor. I could, saith
Martinius, easily grant that all the History of the
Chinois to this very time, is either fabulous, or
comprehends those things, which happened before the flood, whereof the memory might happily be preserved in the Ark. For that many o-
ther things, which appertain also to our faith,
were vindicated from oblivion, and utter destru-
ction even in the same place, is the opinion of
learned men. He farther telleth us, That this
extreme part of *Asia*, whereof we treat, was for
certain inhabited before the flood. But by what
means the memory of things could be preserved
there, when all mankind was wholly destroyed,
if we have not recourse to the family of *Noah*,
is to me, saith the same Author unknown. Hear *Id. pag. 21.*
him. *Hanc enim, qua describo, extremam Asiam,*
ante Diluvium habitatam fuisse pro certo habeo, ve-
rum quo pacto fuerit rerum servata memoria, huma-
no genere omni, si à Noëtica familia discesseris, penitus
deleto, mihi non liquet. And if it should be objected, They might receive the memory of their actions more antient, than the flood by Tradition;
that Tradition also must be acknowledged either,
from *Noah* himself, or some of his sons to have
proceeded.

Of all the Provinces of *China*, *Xensi* for Antiquity hath the preheminence; in regard the
first of Mortals, that ever set footing in *China*
after the Deluge, planted, and took up their first
seats

seats within this Province. To which purpose
Martinius in his Chorography thereof affirms;
That by just right this most noble Province of
Xensi, may with all others the chiefest of this
extreme part of *Asia*, for greatness and Antiquity
contend; for, from times of old, it hath been
the seat of almost all the *Chinique* Emperors, even
from the very original of the *Chinois*, until the
exit of the family of *Hana*, which happened two
hundred sixty four years after the nativity of
CHRIST. And that this Province also, was
the first, as by their most antient Annals appears,
which was inhabited by the first Planters of *China*; and that from the West drawing more into
the East, *They* came thither shortly after the general Deluge of the World; I am, saith he, from
many and those most convincing arguments certainly perswaded.

Observe in like manner, what *Jean Nieuhoff*
in the late Embassage of the Oriental Company
of the United Provinces of the *Netherlands* to the
Emperor of *China* relateth. This Province of

Xensi, saith *Nieuhoff*, is so famous, that for grandeur and Antiquity, it may by just right dispute
with all the Provinces of the Higher *Asia*; for
the Emperors of *China*, have from all times since
the Universal Flood, kept their Imperial residence therein, until the reign of the Family of
Hana. If *Xensi* then be the most antient Countrey of the upper *Asia*, as *Nieuboff* positively asserts; and if of the upper *Asia*, *Babylon* be a Countrey, as all Geographers unanimously affirm, it
follows indisputab'y, that *Xensi* is more antient
than *Babylon*, and consequently received a Colo-

ny

ny into it, before. *Nimrod* and his Troops came into the valley of *Shinaar.*

Now if the credit of their Annals before the flood, fhould be fufpected by us, as they are by the *Chinois* themfelves before the reign of their Emperor *Folins,* we may probably conceive that *Puoncuus* whom they report to be their firft Go-vernor, was the very Conductor of that Colony, that after the Deluge, and before the *Confufion* of Tongues firft came and planted *China.* Neither is authority wanting for the fame. *Indidem licet conjicere omiffis argumentis aliis, Puoncuum & Socios a ceffatione Diluvii, imo ante Turris Babylonicæ molitionem ad Sinas veniffe ;* From whence it may be lawful, faith *Martinius,* to conceive, fetting other arguments afide, that *Puoncuus* and his Af-fociates from the ceffation of the flood, yea, be-fore the Enterprife of the *Babylonian* Tower, came into *China.* When then *China* was planted from the ceffation of the flood, it could not but be much more peopled, ere the Tower was fet in hand, and far more before the *Confufion of Tongues.* For Authors are of opinion, that in re-gard of the vaft greatnefs of the Foundations, and ineftimable quantities of materials requira-ble for the raifing of fuch a prodigious work, in fuch a low and moorifh a Countrey, as *Babylonia* could not but as then be, *Nimrod* and his Confe-derates confumed forty years, before the judg-ment of *confounded* Languages diffolved their work, and difperfed them.

But from thefe his refervations, it may be much fufpected, that *Martinius* in his own thoughts, had an higher opinion of this people,
than

M. Mart. Sin.Hift. Lib.1.p.17.

Sir W.Ral. hift.par.1. pag.100.

than he deemed fitting to be vulgarly made known. And hence happily it is, that *Vossius* saith, *Chorographiæ Sericæ interpres, vir minime ineptus, multo moderatius de gentis hujus virtutibus scripsit, quam sensit ;* The Interpreter of the *Chinique* Chorography, a man that very well understood himself, writ far more moderately of the perfections of this people, than he thought. And therefore had *Martinius,* having in manner from his cradle to his grave studied their Antiquities, written what he thought, and declaring his mind plainly, vouchsafed us those other Arguments he hath concealed, much more no doubt might have been discovered towards the clearing of what ensueth.

For, whether *Puoncuus* was the Ringleader of this first Colony or not, it may be very much presumed, that *Noah* himself both before and after the Deluge lived in *China*. *Josephus* attesteth, that *Noah* having warning of the flood given him from God, seeing his perswasions to repentance and amendment of life, could work no effect upon the Corruption of the Age, and fearing by the violence of the times to perish for his zeal, departed from his native soil, and with his wife and children travelled into another Countrey. *Secedens cum suis in aliam regionem migravit,* saith *Josephus.* Now, why might not this other Region into which *Noah* retired be *China* ? And that confluence of people (which you lately heard of) resort thither, out of desire upon the report of his piety to hear him preach, the better to be prepared against the approaching ruine ? For it seems they repaired thither not only in regard of the

J. Voss. de Ætat. Mun. pag. 45.

Josep. Ant. Jud. lib. 1. cap. 4.

the flood, but also excited by the Fame of the
vertues of *Jaus* and his uprightneſs, throwing
themſelves upon his protection as into their fathers boſome, in ſuch numbers that the then *Chi-*
nique Empire ſcarcely ſufficed to contain them.
From whence we may moreover obſerve, that
the greater the thronging in of their numbers
was, the greater probability there is, they throng-
ed in thither, in hope to ſave themſelves from
the Deluge. Conſidering eſpecially, that the
Chinique Hiſtory recordeth, their Countrey was
at that time deſtroyed by waters, and therefore
Martinius is clearly of opinion, that theſe were
either the waters of *Noahs* flood, which for a
long time after kept the plains and lower places
of this extreme part of *Aſia* overflown, or *China*
was drowned by a peculiar inundation. Hear
him. *Ego malim credere, à Noëtica inundatione ſu-*
perſtites in extremæ hujus Aſiæ planitie, lociſque de-
preſſioribus reſediſſe, aut peculiari eluvie Sinas inun-
datos. But that this Deluge in *China* was not a
peculiar, but the univerſal Deluge, he himſelf
hath verily perſwaded. Hear with him *Semedo*
alſo, maintaining, *Penſano alcui che quell' acque*
erano reliquie del diluvio, That ſome believe theſe
waters were thoſe that remained of the Deluge,
though of their original & encreaſe the *Chinique*
Hiſtory is ſilent. Hear *Voſſius* likewiſe confidently
affirming, *Secundum enim noſtrum calculum dilu-*
vium Sericum exactè cum Noachico convenit, for according to our calculation, ſaith he, the *Serian*
Deluge agrees exactly with the flood of *Noah*.
And it is not to be omitted, that *Jaus*, time being
opportune, ſetting in hand to clear the Countrey

A. Sem.
Rel. del
Cin. par. 1.
pag. 22.

J. Voſ. de
Ætat.
Mun. p. 52.

of

of the Incumbrances which the flood had made, caused the Channels and mouths of the Rivers choaked up, as *Martinius* conceiveth, by the mud and sand which the violence of the Rains of the *Noetique* inundation had brought down, to be opened, and with banks and trenches brought within bounds, about which either through the want of skill in those that he employed, or hands in that newness of the World to assist him, long time was consumed, and not until after many years, during the reigns of his two next ensuing Successors brought to perfection in the end. For the *Chinois* attribute extraordinary Merit unto *Tuus* for the *Adjusting* of these *Waters*, as they call it.

It being then thus, Why might not that other Region into which *Noah* withdrew, be *China*? And this *Jaus*, or *Taus* (for I find the word both by *Martinius*, *Kircherus*, and others indifferently used) be that *Janus* (the middle Letter N added only, gives us the very name, and to cut off the middle Letter, yea, the middle Syllable oftentimes in the proper names of men is and ever hath been usually in the Eastern Languages done) be that *Janus*, I say, whom most Authors maintain was *Noah*? The History that relateth to him, is by *Nieuhoff*, but *Martinius* chiefly, set down in the life of *Taus*, and some circumstances attending it in the reign of his Predecessors; and which as in the most compendious manner, I have thought fitting to present unto you, by the way of Parallel, thus.

First, *Noah* had his name from the *Comfort* his father hoped to receive by him: and *Jaus* had

his

J. Nieuh.
V Amb. Or.
par. 2. pag.
106.
M. Mart.
Sin. hist. lib.
1. p. 3.

his name of the *Happineſſ* his father hoped ſhould proceed from him.

Secondly, *Noah* was ſo juſt and righteous a man, as that he ſurmounted all others of his Age: And *Jaus* ſo excelled in piety and vertue, as that he ſurpaſſed all others of his time.

Thirdly, *Noah* was a *Preacher*, and taught the ways of God. And *Jaus* was a *Divine*, and ordained ſacred Rites, and prayers unto God.

Fourthly, *Noah* was an Husbandman; and *Jaus* preſcribed rules of Husbandry to his people.

Fifthly, In the days of *Noah* the whole World was drowned, and in the days of *Jaus* the whole World was drowned.

Sixthly, Before the flood of *Noah*, was a Conjunction of all the Planets in one Sign; and before the flood of *Jaus* was the like Conjunction of all the Planets.

Seventhly, The ſon of *Noah*, *Cham*, was a reprobate, and therefore by *Noah* made a ſervant to his brethren; and the ſon of *Jaus*, *Chus*, was a reprobate, and therefore by *Jaus* excluded from ſucceſſion in the Empire.

Eighthly and laſtly, the Deluge of *Noah* happened in the year before CHRIST two thouſand two hundred ninety four; and the Deluge that deſtroyed *China* in the time of *Jaus* agrees perfectly therewith; for he began his reign there, in the year before CHRIST two thouſand three hundred fifty ſeven.

Before the time of *Moſes* the name of *Jehovah*, or rather *Haiah*, as *Bayly* in his Practice of Piety obſerves, was never known unto the *Iſraelites*. And thoſe are not wanting that ſuppoſe, that name

*Purch. Pilgrimage,
lib.2.pag.
138.*
name was derived from this *Jaus.* However the *Samaritans,* as I find in *Purchas,* begin their Chronicle after this manner. In the name of *Jah,* the God of *Israel,* there is none like to *Jah* our God, one *Jehova,* God of Gods, Lord of Lords, a great God strong and terrible. *Jah* is my strength and song, saith *Mses* in praysing God for the preservation of *Israel* from the dan-

*Aynswor.
in Exod.*
ger of *Pharaoh,* Exod. 15. v. 2. Wherefore it is not un-observable that the very first utterance that an Infant at his birth yeeldeth is, *ya, ya, ya;* as if the Lord had ordained, either that we should be born with his name *Jah* in our mouths, which name is generally ascribed to him, when some notable deliverance or benefit, according to his former promise comes to pass, because he is the beginning and *Being* of beings, and *giveth to all, life, and breath, and all things,* Act. 17. v. 25. or else, that in our swathling cloathes we should have something of the PRI-MITIVE Language, till afterwards confounded, as we are taught to speak. But by *ya* the *Chinois* intend *Excellens.*

And how long soever the *Chinois* lived undiscovered to other Nations, it seems, that of old, they were not to the *Israelites* unknown, as may be collected from those words of the Prophet *Isaiah,* *Ecce isti a longinquo venient . ecce quoque illi ab Aquilone, & ab Occasu, denique isti à terra Sinæorum;* Behold, these shall come from far: and lo, these from the North and from the West, and these from the land of *Sina. Isai.* 49. v. 12. But when you shall find so many reciprocally mutual customes between them, whether Theology,

logy, or Morality, or what elſe be reſpected, as
throughout our Eſſay ſhall be manifeſted, you
will, without all peradventure, aſſure your ſelves,
that the *Chinois* immediately proceeded from
one and the ſame ſtem *Noah*, as the *Hebrews* originally did, rather than that they ſeem to have
been antiently to one another known.

We may therefore conclude, That if either ſym-
pathy of Qualities, Affinity of names, Coherence
of Times; Concurrence in events; or moſt memorable predictions be of validity in the caſe:
we have at laſt, after ſuch curious enquiry by all
Writers upon this ſubject, and the Plantations
of the World after the Deluge, found out, what
became of *Noah* after he departed out of his native Countrey, and that he lived in *China*. Where
after his deſcent out of the Ark, he might betake
himſelf immediately to his husbandry and planting, in a rich, if not the richeſt ſoil of the whole
Univerſe. And direct his Off-ſpring unto ſuch
parts of the Earth, as either himſelf formerly at
firſt before the flood had lived in, or knew moſt
agreeable to their inclinations, and for their beſt
advantage. Without ever ranging over the
World from *Armenia* to *Arabia Fœlix*, thence into *Africa*, afterwards into *Spain*, and then into
Italy, as *Annius* in his *Beroſus*, and thoſe that follow him, have feigned (*Noah* was an husbandman, no wanderer : ſaith our learned *Raleigh*.) Or without making him to be *Sabazius*
or *Zagreus*, *Prometheus*, *Hercules*, *Ogyges*, *Deucalion*, *Triton*, and I know not who; all men, in
all places, at all times, as *Goropius* would have
him.

But

But we must not leave *Martinius* behind us, in regard especially that how resolved soever he may appear in other matters, we find him confidently positive in and concerning this. Observe him therefore, *Mihi vero religiosum non sit,* Yaum *hunc nostrum eundem cum* Jano *dicere ; ita nominum & temporum affinitate suadente, qui* Janus *multis* Noe *fuisse creditur.* But I may, saith he, without fear assert, that this our *Yaus*, was the same with *Janus*, the affinity of names and times so pervading, which *Janus* is by many conceived to have been *Noah*. Yet how clear soever this Testimony is, let us moreover examine what Authors have said of *Janus*, and by what Character they have found him to be *Noah* ; setting aside their general consent, to which our *Janus* so absolutely corresponds, that they call him *Bifrons*, as seeing and knowing the Ages both before and after the flood.

Of the Antiquity then of *Janus*, *Fabius Pistor* as I find him cited by Sir *W. Raleigh* giveth this testimony. *Jani ætate nulla erat Monarchia, quia mortalibus pectoribus nondum hæserat ulla regnandi cupiditas &c. vinum & far primus populos docuit Janus ad sacrificia: primus enim Aras & Pomœria & Sacra docuit ;* 'In the time of *Janus*, saith he, 'there was no Monarchy, for the desire of rule 'had not then folded it self about the hearts of 'men. *Janus* first taught the people to sacrifice 'wine and meal: he first set up Altars, and in-'stituted gardens and solitary groves, wherein 'they used to pray; with other holy rites and 'ceremonies.

Sir W. Ral.
Histor. par.
1. pag. 91.

Now let us consider how far our *Janus* may
be

be concerned herein ; *Sane si res ab eo gestas recte* **M. Mart.**
expendas , omnes non modo Sinenses, sed orbis fere **Sin. hist.**
totius optimos quosq; reges virtute pariter & gloria vel **lib. 1. p. 36.**
vicit, vel æquavit. Verily, saith *Martinius*, if his actions be truly weighed, as well in vertue, as glory,
he either equalled or excelled, not only all those
of *China*, but all whatever the best Kings, that
almost ever were in the whole World. He lived **J. Nieub.**
in the zeal of Charity ; sowed the seeds of Pray- **l'Amb. Or.**
er ; consulted frequently the highest Divinity ; **par. 2. pag.**
trampled vanity under his feet, gave himself to **106.**
Fastings and Prayers to free his Subjects from
calamities ; and undertook all things with admirable prudence and conduct. But, as near as
possible, we are to observe the *Chinique* phrase, **M. Mart.**
with a celestial piety, and singular wisedome he **Sin. Hist.**
was endued, all welcomed him, as the approach- **lib. 1. p. 37.**
ing Sun ; and by all was expected with as much
desire, as the thirsty fields expect clouds and rain:
He was powerful, but acted just things only ;
Noble and rich, but not proud ; moderate in habit ; temperate in diet ; loved simplicity in saluta-
tions and titles, Rich houshold-stuff he despised,
Pearls and Diamonds contemned ; Venereal en-
ticings not vouchsafe an ear unto ; adorned houses did not inhabit in ; but wearing woollen gar-
ments, with the skins of Deer defended himself
from cold. But, is not this intended , may happily some say, by just *Noah*, whom *Josephus* calls
the Prince of the *Jews*, rather, than pious *Faus*,
the Prince of *China* ? *De religioso potius viro ,*
quam Ethnico Imperatore dicta putes; of a man in holy Orders rather, than an Ethnick Emperour, you
may think them to be spoken, saith *Martinius,*

F However

However we have not 'ended yet, and scarcely can end, his merits are famed to be such. For, he was of surpassing diligence, easie of access to all, never offended with the importunity of any; much less with any incivility, which through ignorance was committed in his presence. He readily heard the differences between his people, and decided them himself; his patience was not to be overcome; his affections not to be moved in treating of Affairs, and in a cool temper with a compassionately moderate voice gave judgment on Malefactors.

And though it is true that Monarchy was then in use amongst the *Chinois*, (For *Fabius Pictor* could not know more, than was then known, and perhaps might think the Terrestrial Globe contained no other Countries, than what were arrived at the *Romans* knowledg) the *desire* nevertheless of *rule*, the World being an Infant and harmless, *had not then folded it self about the hearts of men*. For our *Janus* either weary thereof, or contemning it retired, and confining himself to a solitary grove, lived there in the contemplation of Heaven and Heavenly things; and from the motions of the Cœlestial bodies made such observations, as that his Subjects afterwards became fully instructed by him, not only in the *Institution* of *Gardens*, and *Groves* for their devotions, but also in planting and husbandry of whatever kind was requisite for the benefit of mankind.

Being returned from his solitude (and whether under this solitude may not lie concealed, his going into the Ark, Time is to reveal, it being

ing queſtionable enough. For, *Poſt hæc*, ſaith *Martinius, i. e.* after his having given us the relation
of the abatement of the waters) our *Janus*
brought the *Chinique* Empire into a better, yea,
a new and another kind of form, than formerly it
had, ordaining Sacred Rites, Temples, and Sacrifices; conſtituting Laws both civil and criminal, and appointing ſeveral Tribunals of Juſtice, for the greater eaſe as well of the Subjects,
as their Governours in ſucceeding times, which
continue in full force even at this day. In ſum,
he preſented all things as vertue required, with
ſuch a natural aptneſs, as if goodneſs had been
born with him, *omnia virtute atq; indole quadam ſi-
bi congenita exequebatur*, being my Authors words.
Whereby he filled *China* with his juſt and pious
deeds, and all Ages with his memory; for he
lives a reputed Saint amongſt them at this
day.

He diſinherited his ſon *Chus*, for being (mark
I pray) *Loquax & contentioſus*, a *Pratler* and ſtub-
born, ſaying one thing, acting another, ſeem-
ingly vertuous, really vitious.

After this, he deliberated of his own accord
voluntarily, to make, whilſt living, a reſignation
of his Government, and would have ſurrendred
the ſame to the care of one *Sungous*, who though
of high eſteem for his abilities, pretending nevertheleſs that the charge was too weighty for
him, rejected the ſame. And thereupon our *Janus* reſigned his Dominion to *Xunus*, a right pious, but poor Countryman; who like *Numa* being invited to the Scepter from the plough, lives
as yet no leſs famous for his vertues amongſt

the

the *Chinois*, than *Numa* amongst the *Romans*, but
for his valour much more. I cannot forbear to
remember two principles of his; first, no father
could be so wicked to whom his son owed not
obedience; nor any man so impious, but by instruction and benefits might be induced to lead
an honest and vertuous life.

Now *Martinius* and *Nieuhoff* by their late
search find *Jaus* to have entred upon his Government over *China* about sixty three years before the flood, though *Semedo* in his time will
scarcely allow him twelve. But whether
twelve or five times twelve, they compute, that
he lived both before and after the Deluge, from
which that *Noah* only with his wife, and his sons,
and his sons wives escaped, nothing is more certain. And therefore who this *Taus*, *Jaus*, or
Janus could be, *Noah* excepted, is not to be understood by me, unless happily any shall say, that
the general Deluge happened long before the
year of the World one thousand six hundred fifty six, which I conceive no sober man, if he be
not *Samaritanized* will presume to think. For
the *Samaritans* indeed by diminishing the generations of *Jared*, *Methusalah*, and *Lamech* come
short of the *Hebrew* computation before the
flood, and exceed it much more in the Genealogies of the Patriarchs after the flood.

We are here to observe likewise, that on such
a subject as we now treat of, where the actions
of an Antient people, before these days unto the
Europæans, or more truly, saith *Martinius*, unto
the universal World unknown, are to be enqui-
red into, the more modern Authors are the most

M. Mart:
Sin. hist. in
Epist. Dedic

warrant-

warrantable. For heretofore their Histories were reputed meer Fables, even by men of judgment, insomuch as *Lodovicus Vives* (living about the time of their first discovery) writes, that he wonders how any man could spend his time about such trifles.

Although their Histories be true, Historiæ illorum, licet sint veræ, saith *Vossius.* For, since the *Tartarian* War, as if Divine Power had decreed, they should be conquered to this end; *Their* discovery is generally compleated; *Their* Antiquity certainly known; *Their* Language plainly understood, so far in present at least, as conduceth to our enquiry; *Time* being to make known the rest. For, now free conversation is permitted, and full liberty granted to study in any of *Their* Libraries at pleasure, and to buy and imprint any of *Their* Books; which when at first the Jesuites began to collect, was by publique Edict prohibited. Insomuch, that if we diligently make use, of what is Providentially cast upon us, we shall not only not need much longer to be inquisitive wherein *Their* Learning consisteth, but also find their Language to be, as the most antient, so the most delightful and harmless, of all others at this day known throughout the World. *Hoc demum ævo Serum calamitas, Serum nobis dedit notitiam,* now at last in this our Age, the calamity of the *Chinois,* hath given us knowledg of the *Chinois.* As the same *Vossius* hath it.

In what part of the World *Noah* built the Ark, the Scriptures are altogether silent; nor hath any approved Author, *Goropius Becanus* set aside, written thereof. Only this we are assured

If. Vos. Æt at. Mun. pag. 45.

Id. pag. 46.

F 3 of

of, that the Ark was built, not in the North, or Northwest, but in that part of the World which lay East from *Shinaar* : And to my under-

Sir *W. Ral.*
hist. par. 1. p.
93.

standing, saith Sir *W. Raleigh*, not far from the place, where it rested after the flood ; for *Noah* did not use either Mast or Sail (as in other Ships) and therefore did the Ark no otherwise move, than the hulk or body of a Ship doth in a calm Sea. Also because it is not probable, that during those continual and downright rains there were any winds at all ; therefore was the Ark little moved from the place, where it was fashioned, and set together. For it is written, *God made a wind to pass upon the Earth, and the waters ceased.* Gen. 8. v. 1. From whence it may be gathered, that during the fall of the waters, there was not any storm or forceable wind at all, which could drive the Ark any great distance from the place, where it was first by the waters lifted up. Thus far that Noble Gentleman.

Goropius Becanus in his *Indo-Scythia* doth in maintenance of his opinion, that the Ark took ground upon the mountains of *Caucasus*, suppose, that *Noah* built the Ark near those mountains, because on those hills are goodly Cedars : and that to this place *Noah* repaired both to separate himself from the reprobate Giants, who rebelled against God and Nature, as also because he would not be interrupted in building of the Ark ; to which also he addeth conveniency of Rivers to transport the Timber, which he used without troubling any other carriages. Whereby *Goropius* appears you see very careful to supply *Noah* with necessaries for so great a work ;

and

and considering his giving so near a conjecture, as he doth, at the place where the Ark might rest, he had great reason to fortifie the same, with as many circumstances, as the quality of that Clime would admit.

But having discovered such manifest footsteps of the Residence of *Noah* in *China*, after he withdrew from the corruption of the World, as that they far outweigh whatever supposal to the contrary; we must now wave *Caucasus*, and confidently affirm, that no Countrey, in the habitable Earth could better furnish *Noah*, with all manner of conveniences, and every sort of materials proper for the building of such a Machine than *China*. For, if the Ark were made of Pine-trees, as the *Geneva* translation renders the word *Gopher*, then *Kircherus* will assure you, such Pine-trees are in *China*, that eight men can scarcely fathom them, and that thirty eight men may stand within the body of them. If according to the Rabbins of Cedar, then *Purchas* will tell you, that their store is such, as the *Chinois* use Cedar for funeral coffins and Tombs. If as the *Septuagint* of square timber, or as the *Latine* of smooth timber, then *Nieuhoff* affirms, that of all kind of trees for Carpenters work, such plenty, and of such several sorts is to be found within that Empire, that the number is beyond admiration incredible.

And as for conveniency of Rivers to transport the Timber, though without the use of other carriages, it could never be brought to be put in work, either by *Noah* or his Assistants; *Caucasus* must with *Goropius* his good favour give place

A. Kirch. Ch. Ill. par. 4. p. 185.

Purch. Pilgrim age, lib. 4. pag. 438.

J. Nieuh. l' Amb: Or. par. 2. p. 80

to

to *China*; for therein may be numbred no leſs, than an hundred and eleven Rivers, ſome of them reſembling Seas rather, than navigable ſtreams; ſo that, ſaith *Kircherus*, there is ſcarcely a field but is watered by them; whereby the whole Empire is almoſt every where paſſable by boat, ſaith *Martinius*. Whereas *Caucaſus* can boaſt of the ſpring-heads only of three, thoſe nevertheleſs very famous ones, *Indus*, *Hydaſpes*, and *Zuradrus*; and though *Oxus* is ſaid to have his ſpring on the North-ſide of *Caucaſus*, as thoſe other on the South; the mountains notwithſtanding are ſo inacceſſible, as no timber could any way by whatever humane help be tranſported, from that part. But *Kircherus* by a late diſcovery finds *Indus*, together with *Ganges*, *Ravi*, and *Aibec* the greateſt Rivers of all *India* to have their firſt beginnings in the mountains of the Kingdom of *Thebeth*, above one hundred leagues from *Caucaſus*, whereby *Goropius* for confirmation of his opinion, comes to be utterly deprived of the conveniency of the chiefeſt of all his Rivers.

Beſides, as careful as he was, he hath wholly forgotten to furniſh *Noah* at Mount *Caucaſus* with pitch; for according to the peremptory command, *He was to* make the Ark, and pitch it within and without, with pitch. *Gen. 6. v. 14.* Whereof Sir *W. Raleigh* taking good notice, and well knowing the command being ſo poſitive, was not to be neglected, ſaith, " That the pitch " which *Noah* uſed, is by ſome ſuppoſed to have " been a kind of *Bitumen*, whereof there is great " quantity about the valley of *Sodome*, and *Gomorra*; now the dead Sea or *Aſphaltes*, and in the
Region

" Region of *Babylon*, and in the Weſt *India*. But
I muſt with all reſpect neverthleſs, to ſo celebrated an Author, ſay, that the neareſt of
theſe places from the *Caucaſian* mountains of *A-
rarat* is diſtant about ſeven hundred leagues, and
therefore ſomewhat too far, as I conceive at leaſt,
for *Noah* to tranſport ſuch quantities of *Bitumen*,
as he was of neceſſity to uſe upon ſo important
an occaſion. Now, of the great ſtore of pitch
that *China* affordeth, no more aſſured teſtimony
can be given, than *Their* multitudes of Shipping,
and infinite number of Pine-trees; but that kind
of pitch which theſe trees produceth, and which
is to us ſo welcome; the *Chinois* have in little
eſteem; But uſe and ever did, a bituminous or
pitchy ſubſtance found in great abundance every
where throughout *Their* Countrey, which they
make up, as we do morter with the oyl of a certain fiſh, and therewith calk and dreſs their
Ships. This pitch of *Theirs*, as *Gonſalez Mendoza* G. *Mend.*
in his Hiſtory of *China* relates, is not only more *hiſt. del Chi.*
tenacious than ours, but alſo breedeth few worms *lib.3.pag.*
(a matter of no ſmall importance in thoſe Seas) 167.169.
and makes the timber endure like ſtone. So that
one Ship of *Theirs* will out-laſt two of ours,
and did they not build them thin, would laſt
much longer.

Neither doth *Goropius* acquaint us, how *Noah*
in thoſe barbarous and deſolate upland Countries
confining *Caucaſus*, came by workmen to aſſiſt
him; for himſelf and family, without the help
of Angels, or the like miracle, could never of
themſelves have accompliſhed ſuch a Fabrick.
Whereas the natural ingenuity of the *Chinois*
might

might not only give him affistance, but advife alfo, in what manner to put in work the directions
that God had given him for building of the Ark;
which if it were made in that part of the World
which lay Eaft from *Shinaar*, as moft certainly it
was, then no Countrey under the Sun can be
found more Eaftward from thence than *China*.

The Vines which grow about Mount *Caucafus*, are much celebrated both by Sir *W. Raleigh*
and *Goropius*, they ufing them as a principal argument, for the refting of the Ark there. But if e-
ver in any part of the habitable Earth the Vine
grew naturally, it is in *China* in the Province of
Xenfi efpecially; but in *Xanfi*, faith *Martinius*,
are the moft delicious grapes of all others in *China*; where in the City of *Pingyang* their never
enough by them extolled Emperour *Faus* refi-
ded, So that, as Sir *W. Raleigh* obferves of *Noah*,
he needed not *to travail far to feek out the Vine*;
when it grew at his very door. But though they
have Vines in all abundance, and fuch as yeeld
moft delicious fruit, the *Chincis* neverthelefs de-
fpife the wine thereof, and drying up the grapes
for Rayfins make a wine of Rice, no lefs generous and noble than ours, ftieping therein the
flefh of Kidds, I know not, faith *Martinius*, with
what Art prepared. It is highly efteemed by the
Chinois, hath an excellent body, is very ftrong,
and grateful to the taft and pleafant. They make
it not of ordinary Rice; but a certain kind of
it peculiar to their Countrey, which ferveth only to make this liquor.

And as for that, that *Goropius* faith, the Ark
rested

*A. Sem.
Rel. del
Cin. par.1.
c. 1.
M.Mart.
Atl.Sin.
pag.39,41.*

*J.Nieu.
l'Amb.Or.
par.2.p.88.*

rested upon the mountains of *Caucasus*, because
of all others it is the highest mountain in the
World, it is no argument at all; unless it could
be made appear, that, as it is feigned of the *Argos*,
the Ark had sence to direct it self, or *Noah* a rud-
der to steer it thither. It may as well be said,
that it took ground on the Pike of *Tenariff*,
which is conceived neither to yeeld to *Caucasus*,
or any other whatever hill in the Universe for
height. This we are certain of, that the Ark rested on the Mountains, and reason granteth it was
such a Mountain, as, were it more or less high,
after the abatement of the waters, the Ark first
touched upon; and setling afterwards as they
declined, firmed on the same. And therefore
nor Scripture nor reason will allow, it should be
the highest of all others.

However, if need require, *China* will afford
us mountains of inaccessible altitude; for *Kirche-* | *A. Kir. Ch.*
rus tells us, That this Empire is adorned with | *Ill.par.4.*
innumerable hills; some of them being in regard | *p.169,170.*
of their immense height cloathed with perpe-
tual serenity, others again covered with a continual obscurity of hovering clouds. The greatest
and highest especially, the *Chinois* have in so great
veneration, as that they are transported with no
study more, than a vain observation of them,
supposing all their felicity and fortune to consist
in them. And why? because the Dragon, whom
they make the Lord of felicity inhabites them.
But in regard many things are now done whereof the original cause is hardly to be conjectured,
I should, were it lawful for me to interpose
herein, conceive rather, that this their impu-
ting

ting all their happiness and prosperity to their
mountains, might at first proceed from the felicity and good fortune they attained, by their
Anceftors being at the time of the flood preferved in the Ark upon fuch mountains; great deliverances having in all times, amongft all Nations, by feveral ways, with reference neverthelefs to the occafion been commemorated. Thus
the *Ifraelites* obferved the Paffeover, in remembrance that their forefathers were paffed over,
and faved, when all the firft-born of *Ægypt* were
flain. And I forget not to have read, That fome
are of opinion, the *Nemæan* Games were by the
Græcians folemnized, becaufe *Hercules* flew the
Nemæan Lion, though others with more authority affert, they were folemnized in regard of
the prefervation of *Adraftus* and his Army, that
in their march towards *Thebes* had all perifhed
in the foreft of *Nemæa,* if they had no been preferved by *Hypfiphile* who directed them to a
fountain of water there. And thofe alfo are not
wanting, that fuppofe the *Lupercalia* were inftituted by the *Romans* in honour of *Pan*, when
more probably they were inftituted in memory
that their Founders *Romulus* and *Remus* were faved by being fuckled and brought up by *Lupa* the
wife of *Fauftulus.* And that, from the prefervation of their Anceftors, as we faid, this fuperftition of the *Chinois* may proceed, is not altogether
unwarrantable, but attended with a moft remarkable circumftance. For by their Hiftory it
appears,that at the time when *China* was drowned, fome people were faved upon the mountain
Feu neer the City of *Kaocheu* in the Province

of

of *Quantung.* Which from *Martinius* you may *M. Mart. At Sin. pag. 139.* receive thus. *Feu mons ad ortum urbis tantæ altitudinis, ut hunc eluvionis Sinicæ tempore, vertice super aquas eminuiſſe velint, in eoque homines aliquot ſalvos perſtitiſſe & incolumes.* Hear the same confirmed by *Nieuhoff* also, *Si nous voulions croire le* *J. Nieuh. l' Amb. Or. par. 1. p. 89.* *Chinois, nous dirions que Kaocheu, ſeptiéme ville de Quantung, avoiſine une montagne, nommée de Feu, qui pour ſa hauteur incomparable ſervit d' Aſyle, & de port à pluſieurs hommes durant le deluge ;* If we may credit the *Chinois*, they will tell us, saith he, that *Kaocheu* the seventh City of *Quantung*, hath adjoyning to it a Mountain called *Feu*, which being of incomparable height served for an *Aſylum* and Port to several men during the Deluge. Now, why might not these, thus saved, be *Noah* and his family, though no mention of the Ark be made, or its taking Port there ? Conſidering, that They only escaped the Deluge; that the *Chinique* Deluge was the same with *Noah*'s; and that by what means the memory of things, both before and at the flood, ſhould be preſerved amongſt the *Chinois*, when all mankind was wholly deſtroyed, without having recourſe to *Noah* and his family, is unknown. But my conjecture is ſcarcely delivered, when an objection is caſt in my way.

For it is now said, That if *Noah* lived in *China* before the flood, how could the Ark reſt upon the mountains of *Ararat*, as the Scripture ſaith poſitively, it did ; when *Caucaſus* being a mountain of *Ararat* is diſtant from *China* at leaſt four hundred leagues, and when the Ark having neither Sails to carry it, Oars to row it, nor current

rent to drive it, could, as hath been said, hull up
and down only, as on a standing pool? And therefore it may be much more probable, that *Noah*
both lived and built the Ark not far from the
Mountains of *Caucasus*, where it took ground,
as Sir *W. Raleigh*, and *Goropius* have supposed.
To this is answered, That in the Province of *Ly-*
cia, a Region of *Asia minor* near the *Mediterra-*
nean Sea, that ledge of Hills begins, which *Moses*
calleth *Ararat*, now known by the name of *Tau-*
rus, and which running through the lesser and
greater *Asia*, not far from *Caucasus* meets with
Heyl.Cosm. the Mount *Imaus*. Now, though the Antient
pag.796. Writers could trace the course of this Mountain
A.Kirc.Ch.
Ill.par.1. no farther, yet later observations follow it to
pag.46. the wall of *China*; and find, that the main body
M.Mart. of it, having held on an even course from West
Atl.Sin.p.1.
J.Nieuh. to East, and there dividing, one ridge bounds
l'Amb.Or. *China* on the West, and the other continueth on
par.1.p.11. the North thereof, even through *Corea* until it
Ort.p.106. encounters with the East Sea there. And this not
only all the modern, and therefore perfect Geographical Descriptions of this extreme part of
Asia will testifie, but hereof *Heylin* also, who hath
been as diligent in the search thereof, as any,
Heyl.Cosm. shall assure you : his words being ; "*China* is
p.864. "bounded on the North with *Altay*, and the East-
"ern *Tartars*, from which separated by a conti-
"nued chain of Hills, part of those (mark I
"pray) of *Ararat*. Whereby it appears, that as
Ararat had its *Caucasus*, so *China* had her *Ararat*,
upon which the Ark might rest, as upon the
mountains of *Ararat*, the Scripture saith positively it did. And it is not un-observable, the
Scripture

Scripture teacheth us, that the Ark refted, not
on the mountain in the fingular, but on the
mountains of *Ararat* in the plural. A manifeft
argument that *Ararat* was a general name, and
had reference to the whole ledge of Hills, not to
any particular mountain fo called. As we even
at this day both in difcourfe and writing ufe in
the fame fence to fay, not the mountain, but
mountains of *Taurus*; not the *Pyrænian* hill,
but hills; not the *Alp*, but *Alps*. Neither
muft we forget, that if according to the *Hebrew*
mode you caft your eye from the right to the
left, and admit *Taura* in the *Fæminine*, you fhall
find it will produce *Aruat*. And had *Goropius*
lived to have perufed our late difcoveries, he
would never fo contrary to reafon, have raifed, I
know not how changeable and violent winds to
drive the Ark from the fouth of *Paropamifus* into the north to the beginning of *Caucafus*, and
then back to the fouthward again, until at laft
upon the higheft tops of *Caucafus*, by great good
fortune, he makes it reft. Nor he, or our *Raleigh*
troubled themfelves and Readers, with fo many
tedious Arguments about this Mountain as they
have done, but without doubt, have concluded,
that the Ark refted on the mountains of *Ararat*
confining *China*. In which Region *Noah* having
lived before the flood, the Ark needed neither
Winds, nor Sails, nor Oars, nor Current to
tranfport it; but being born up by the waters,
might in five moneths time, going upon them,
be wafted by the weight of them only, let the
pool be as ftanding as you pleafe, out of the plain
Countrey of *China* below, to the adjoyning
moun-

*G. Bec. In-
def. p. 456.*

mountains of *Ararat* above, And thereby both
sacred Scripture fulfilled, and prophane History
certainly reconciled.

For, thus with the Scripture, *Nimrod* and his
Troops might go from the East to the valley of
Shinaar, as the very letter of the Text saith
they did; whereas *Caucasus* bendeth into the
North. *And as they journeyed from the East, they
found a plain in the land of Shinaar, and they
dwelt there.* As if the Providence of God had decreed, that the World should begin to be planted, even from the utmost extremity thereof,
thereby to prescribe a rule to all after Ages; in
what manner they ought to conduct and carry
on their Plantations by degrees. Hence as it was
with our forefathers, so by us in the setling of Colonies, it is still observed, to follow always the
Sun, wheresoever it is free, and may without
danger be done, lest otherwise the conduct of
Nature should seem without cause to be resisted
by us.

Thus with *Raleigh*, *Noah*, at first when he
came down out of the Ark after returning thanks
to God for his deliverance, might become an husbandman, no wanderer; *Nimrod* be six years in
travailing from the place, where the Ark rested
to *Shinaar*; and *India* the sooner inhabited by
the way thither, whereby the vast numbers of
the army of *Staurobates*, with which he encountred *Semiramis*, might have sufficient time to be
propagated, and consequently exceed hers.
Thus, with the same Author, *Goropius* and *Heylin*,
the Ark might rest not far from the place where
Noah lived, without calling sometimes the
                                    North,

North, sometimes the South winds to help, as *Goropius* doth; and *Noah* be setled in the East, and have well peopled all those parts, which lay nearest to him, before he sent *Nimrod* and his Troop abroad to search for other habitations. Thus with *Raleigh* also, might the sons of *Joctan* left behind with *Noah*; orderly and quietly be planted in the several Regions of *India* beyond *Ganges*: Whereas otherwise, being, as is conceived, they were not born, till after the *Confusion* of *Tongues*, they could not possibly pass from *Babel* with their families, flocks, and herds of cattle into such remote parts, through the interjacent Kingdoms, fully peopled, and after the dispersion long before they could be of Age to wander, all full of wars and tumults. Thus with *Heylin* might *China* be planted before the rest of the Adventurers went to seek new fortunes at the Tower of *Babel*. Thus, with *Martinius* might *Jaus* without scruple be *Noah*, this extreme part of *Asia* wherof we write, be for certain inhabited before the flood; the History of *China* preserved in the Ark; and the people thereof arrive to the perfection of Arts and Sciences, so early as they did. Thus, with *Willet* might *Noah* without dispute be exercised in planting of Religion, and doing most excellent works for the benefit of Mankind; Thus, with *Nieuhoff* might *Xensi* be of just right the most antient Province of *Asia*, and in memory thereof the Emperours of *China* keep their Imperial residence therein, ever since the universal Flood, till the reign of the family of *Hana*. Thus, with *Heylin* and *Martinius* both, might *China* unquestionab'y be peopled from

G the

the ceſſation of the Deluge, before the Enterpriſe of *Babel* , and *Confuſion* of *Tongues.* And
thus may the Language of the Empire of *China*
be preferred to all others.

And hereby we find , that Sir *W. Raleigh* had
great reaſon to aſſert , That theſe Eaſtern parts
of the World were the firſt peopled Countries
after the flood , and planted before *Noah* ſent
Nimrod and his followers abroad upon new diſ-
coveries. And that *Heylin* might upon good
grounds conceive, that *China* was primitively
planted by ſome of the Poſterity of *Sem* before
the Undertaking at *Babel*" Which may probably
" be concluded, ſaith he, from the extreme popu-
" louſneſs of the Countrey , the many magnifi-
" cent Cities, their Induſtry and Ingenuity in all
" Arts and Sciences , not to be taught them by
" their neighbours more ignorant in thoſe things
" than themſelve. *Et ſane totius Indiæ populos Si-*
nis circumjacentes mere barbaros incultoſque dixe-
ris, ſi cum Sinis comparentur : And verily , ſaith
Martinius, you may ſay, that all the people of *In-*
dia confining *China* are meerly rude and barbarous, in compariſon of the *Chinois.* And the reaſon, wherefore the farther Eaſt ſhould be the
more civil ; Sir *W. Raleigh* hath long ſince told
us, is, becauſe it had *Noah* himſelf for an Inſtruct-
er. But unto thoſe Excellencies of the *Chinois,*
we ſhall add their Antient Theology alſo.

CHINA of all Kingdoms the moſt vaſt and
greateſt, is, according to the late Geography en-
vironed on the Eaſt with the Oriental Sea, on the
North ſeparated from *Tartaria antiqua,* the
Realms of *Niuche, Niulhan,* and part of *Tangia*
by

Heyl. Coſm.
p.870.

M. Mart.
Sin. Hiſt.
lib.6.p.237

A Kirch.
Ch. III.par.
1.pag.3.

by a vaſt wall, of which had the Antients had
knowledg, they would without doubt have celebrated amongſt their other Wonders of the
World. On the Weſt it is ſurrounded partly
with a ridg of moſt high hills, partly with the
ſandy deſart of *Zamo*, and ſeveral Kingdoms;
and on the South the Meridional Ocean with the
Kingdoms of *Tunching*, *Cochin-China*, *Lao*, and
others bound it. *Semedo* ſaith, it is as big as
Spain, *France*, *Italy*, *Germany*, the *Low-Countries*,
Great Britain, and all the Iſlands belonging to it.
According to *Martinius*, it extends in Longitude
about thirty degrees, from the Head or Ptomon-
tory of the City of *Ningpo* (called by the *Portugals Liampo*) as far as to the *Amaſæan* or *Dama-
ſian* mountains. The greateſt Latitude is from
the eighteenth degree to the fortieth ſecond of
the North Hemiſphere. Whereby, the figure of
it, as *Nieuhoff* hath it, tendeth to a ſquare form,
being four hundred and fifty German Leagues
length, and three hundred and thirty in bredth.
But in all this mighty Continent are no ſuch
waſte grounds or un-habitable Deſarts as in
other Countries, but full of goodly Towns and
Cities.

The Provinces of this Empire are fifteen, and
in almoſt every one of them, more men fit for
War to be found, than in all *England* and *Scotland*. Inſomuch; that if the firſt bleſſing con-
ferred on Mankind both before and after the
flood of *Encreaſe and multiply*, Gen. 1. v. 28. Gen.
9. v. 1. was ever to this day conſpicuous in any
Nation under Heaven, it is manifeſtly viſib'e in
this. For, by the Rolls in which the number of

Marginal notes:

*A. Sem.
Rel. del
Cin. par. 1.
pag. 20.
M. Mart.
Atl. Sin.
pag. 2.*

*F. Nieuh.
l' Amb. Or.
par. 1. pag.
41.*

People is regiftred, appears, that there are there-in ten Millions, two hundred eight thoufand five hundred fixteen families ; and fifty eight Millions, nine hundred fourteen thoufand, two hundred eighty four fighting men ; befides, the Royal family, Magiftrates, Eunuch's, Garrifon-Souldiers, Priefts, women and children, which are not numbred in the Regifters of the Provinces. Thus *Nieuhoff* cafteth up the account, from whom *Martinius* and *Kircherus* do not much vary. And therefore we need not wonder, that the *Portugals* at their firft arrival in *China*, beholding fuch fwarms of people in every place, demanded, if their women there brought forth nine or ten children at a birth.

A. Kirc.
Ch. Ill. par.
4. pag. 167, 168.

And leaft fuch multitudes fhould be deftitute of habitations, there are within the Empire one hundred and fifty Metropolitane Cities, furpaf-fing all others in magnificence and reputation ; and of a leffer degree, twelve hundred twenty fix, all fortified with walls and ditches ; befides Caftles, Fortreffes, Burgoifes, Towns, Hamlets, Villages, of which there is no number. So that at the end of every mile at leaft, new and new habitations appear. All the Cities neverthelefs are built after one form, *viz.* of a fquare figure, and he that hath feen one of them, may eafily comprehend the manner of all the reft. The hou-fes are for the moft part of Timber, and gene-rally of one ftory high, whereby as they avoid the wearying of themfelves in afcending by ftairs, fo they take up much ground, what they want in height being fully recompenced by the length. They are, without rude, but within
                                                    adorned

adorned with all manner of splendour and magnificence. Thus *Kircherus.*

But our *Heylin* more particularly proceedeth, *Heyl.Cosm.*
finding *China* to be provided with five hundred *pag.864.*
ninety one Cities, fifteen hundred ninety three
walled Towns, eleven hundred fifty four Castles,
four thousand two hundred Towns unwalled,
and such a number of Villages, that the whole
Countrey seemeth to be but one City. Besides,
their dwellings on Shipboard, wherein
whole families reside, and where they buy, sell,
are born, live and die. In such numbers, as that
the question may well be, saith *Kircherus*, whether more people live aboard their Ships, or in *A.Kirch.*
the Countries and Cities, those especially that *Ch.Ill.par.*
are on the Sea-coasts. And of Shipping such *5.p.216.*
multitudes they have, that the Rivers seem to be
no otherwise covered with them, than the land
with houses; whence the *Chinois* use, by way of
Proverb to say, that their Emperour is able to
make a Bridge of Ships from *China* to *Malaca,*
which are five hundred Leagues asunder. And
least any that tow the Vessels in course of Trade,
should be obstructed or retarded in their passage,
neither any Tree is suffered to grow, or other
impediment permitted within five foot of the
water-side. And the same order is observed for
the better commoding of the highways to the
use of Travellers.

But I cannot moreover desist from *Kircherus* *Id.in Epist.*
his farther description thereof. It is, saith he, of *Ded.*
such greatness of Power, that in the circumference
of the Earthly Globe, a more mighty Monarchy,
and more populous cannot comparable there-

G 3 unto

unto be found. The Kingdom of *China* alone, we
may see so adorned with innumerable, and those
most flourishing Cities, that if we should say, it
were one entire Province, we should hardly say
amiss. It is so furnished with frequent Towns,
Castles, Villages, and places dedicated to their
superstition; that if that wall of three hundred
leagues in length, memorable in all Ages, were
extended from Sea to Sea, all *China* throughout,
how great, how large soever, might not unde-
servedly be said to be one City, in which is found
such infinite plenty of whatever is necessary for
the life of mankind; as that, that which the
wise industry of Nature hath here and there a-
monst other Kingdoms of the World dispersed, may all be summarily seen to be contained within this one only.

I could acquaint you also, that the revenue of
their Emperour amounteth yearly unto one hundred and fifty millions of Crowns, and how it is
raised, and disposed of; but I forbear, more important matters as to our present disquisition,
calling on me to proceed unto their *Theology* of
old, before they became infected with Idolatry.

J. Nieuh.
L. Amb: Or:
par. 2. pag.
54. Amongst all the Nations of the Universe, the
Chinois have most avoided to be guided by the
light of Nature, & least erred in the rules of their
Religion; For, we know with what prodigious
follies, the Descendents of *Cham* and *Japhet*, the
Greeks, *Romans*, and *Ægyptians* heretofore stuffed
their Divine Worship. When the *Chinois* on the
contrary, have, from immemorable times ever
acknowledged one only God, whom they name
the Monarch of *Heaven*. And we may find, saith
Nieuhoff,

Nieuhoff, by their Annals for more than four, thousand years, that in this particular, there were never Pagans that less offended. Whereby the rest of their Actions are the more conformable to that which right reason requires. And here-with *Nicholaus Trigantius* in his Christian Expedition into *China* fully consents.

But let us see what *Martinius* will afford us. Of the Great and first Author of things, saith he, there is amongst all the *Chinois* a wonderful silence, for, in so copious a Language God hath not so much as a name ; oftentimes nevertheless they use the word *Xangti*, by which they signifie the Supream Governour of Heaven and Earth. This *Numen*, we may say, was the *Tetragrammaton* of the *Chinois* ; *Deus Optimus Maximus* being, as is generally conceived, professed and adored by them of old under the name of *Xangti*. *Huic enim ut supremo numini sacra faciebant, fundebantque preces, nullis ad religionem exciendam simulacris aut statuis usi ; quippe qui numen ubique præsens venerantes, illud extra sensus omnes positum, nulla crederent imagine posse mortalium oculis repræsentari.* For unto him as to the supreme God they offered sacrifices and poured forth their prayers, using neither Statues nor Images for stirring up their devotion ; for in regard adoring an Omnipotent and Incomprehensible Deity, they believed he was not by the resemblance of any thing to be represented to the eyes of Mortals. Now by whom could this people be instructed in such divine principles as these, but by *Noah* or *Sem* ? For certain we are that the *Hebrews* who descended from *Noah* and *Sem* held it unlawful

N. Trig. in Chi. Exp. apud Sin. lib.1.p.104

M. Mart. Sin. Hist. Lib.1.p.11.

Id. lib.4. pag.149.

G 4

to

to use the name *Jehovah*, except within the Sanctuary, when the Priest blessed the People, according to the Law, in *Num. 6.v. 23.* And that they were *not to make unto Him any graven Image, or any likeness of any thing, that is in Heaven above, or that is in the Earth beneath, or that is in the water under the Earth*; we find in *Exod. 20. v.4.*

But *Martinius* will conduct us farther yet. In these our days they worship a certain *Numen*, which what it is, they verily know not. As, the *Athenians*, I may add, had an Altar dedicated unto the unknown God, which as the Apostle instructeth us, was God that made Heaven and Earth. *Act. 17. v.24.* But that of old, saith *Martinius*, the *Chinois* professed the true God, from the Doctrine delivered them by *Noah*, there is no doubt to be made. *Olim vero quin verum Deum agnoverint, ex doctrina Noë tradita dubium nobis nullum est*; Being his words.

M. Mart.
in hist. lib.
2. p. 333.

They have an opinion, that many go erring in the mountains that never die, and fly like Spirits ascending up to Heaven, when they please; which *Martinius* inclines to conceive is grounded on the History of *Enoch* and *Elijah*.

Id. lib. 4.
p. 145.

They were not without some knowledge of CHRIST, as the Books written by their Philosopher *Confutius*, stiled the *Plato* of the *Chinois* is manifest; he being an Author of as sublime and profound Authority with them, as either *Plato* or *Aristotle* with us; and indeed more antient. *Confutium prævidisse VERBUM carnem futurum, idque non dubia se præcepisse, quin & annum in Cyclo Sinico, quo futurum esset cognovisse;*
Confutius,

Confutius, faith our Author, forefaw that the
WORD fhould become flefh, and not only confidently taught it, but knew in what year of the
Chinique Cycle it fhould come to pafs. (The Cycle of *China* to remember it by the way, containeth fixty years, as the Olympiad of the
Greeks did four.) And it is memorable, that their
Emperour that reigned at the birth of CHRIST *Id.lib.io.*
would not be called *Ngayus*, as his name was, *pag.413.*
but *Pingus*, which fignifies *Pacificns*; by a wonderful Providence of God, that at the time that
CHRIST the true *Pacifique* King came upon
the Earth, the Emperour of *China* fhould be
called *Pacifique* alfo.

I find in *Purchas*, that *Nicolao di Conti* relateth, *Pur. Pil-*
that when the *Chinois* rife in the morning, they *grimago,*
turn their faces to the Eaft, and with their hands *lib.4.pag.*
joyned, fay, *God in Trinity keep us in his Law.* But *460. Nic.*
in regard it doth not fully appear that from An- *pud Ra-*
tiquity they have ufed the fame, and that *Marti-* *muf.*
nius is filent therein, we fhall not infift upon
it.

To return therefore to *Confutius*, his ufual
faying, and wherein he concluded, the higheft
perfection to confift, was, *Ne facias ulli, quod pati*
nolis, which is the Law and the Prophets. *And*
as you would that men fhould do to you, do ye alfo to
them likewife. Luk.6.v.31. Mat.7.v.12. And *M. Mart.*
though he flourifhed before CHRIST above *Sin.Hift.*
five hundred years, many of his off-fpring, never- *lib.4.p.137*
thelefs, are yet remaining and live in great ho-
nour, at this day; which is worthy obfervation
it being not to be faid again of any family in any
place under Heaven except in *China* : where indeed

deed many more like instances may be found, that especially of the now Princes of *Corea*, they being lineally descended from *Kicius*, who in the year one thousand one hundred twenty two before the Incarnation of CHRIST, had for his eminent learning, that Kingdom given him in reward by *Faus* the first Emperour of *China*, of the family of *Cheva*. Whereby it appears that the Posterity of *Kicius*, have in a continued succession enjoyed the Kingdom of *Corea*, two thousand seven hundred and ninety years.

Id Lib.i.
p.13,14.

The most learned Philosophers amongst the *Chinois*, make the *Chaos* the beginning and original of all things; out of which the highest *Immaterial* or spiritual *Being* created that, that is material. They hold also, that the World was created in the winter Solstice; the Heavens first, the Earth next, then living Creatures, lastly, Man. After the same manner, as *Moses* hath delivered. *Gen.* I.

That the World shall be dissolved into the *Chaos*, from whence it came, and that before the dissolution thereof, there shall be great perturbation of all orders, and all things; with mighty Wars, insurrections of Kingdoms, and from thence publique calamities shall arise throughout the universal Globe, they are clearly of opinion. Now, how fully they accord with the words of our Saviour herein. *Matth.* 24. *v.*6,7. declares.

M. Mart.
Sin. hist.
lib.1. p. 11.

Add unto these, that in their Books they frequently assert, rewards to be decreed for vertue, and punishments for vice. But this seems only to relate unto the condition of our present life; for that they have any knowledge of the Judgment

ment hereafter, from *Martinius* appears not. The Antiquity of their *Theology* not conducting them so far. Yet neverthelefs I find in *Trigantius*, that from all times they have made no queſtion of the immortality of the Soul, ſpeaking often of the dead, as living in Heaven, but of the puniſhments of wicked men in Hell, not a word.

N. Trig. in *Chriſt. Exp.* *apud Sin.* *lib.* 1. *p.* 105.

The name of *Juſtice* they confine not to that vertue which is a conſtant and perpetual will of giving every man his due. But allow it ſuch a latitude that every action conſentaneous to reaſon is thereby ſignified. A true Maxime; for whatever is agreeable to reaſon, we may juſtly ſay to be juſt. And by the name of *Piety* they underſtand not the love only of God, their Parents, or themſelves, but of all men univerſally. For, as they define *Juſtice* to be the law and conveniency of doing well; ſo *Piety*, the means and rule of loving well. A Divine Principle, for we are to love our neighbours as our ſelves; according to that in *Matth.* 22. *v.* 39.

M. Mart. *Sin. Hiſt.* *lib.* 3. *p.* 96.

Now, this high Divinity of *Theirs* admits a particular reflexion. *H. Grotius* in his diſcourſes of God and his Providence, as I find him Engliſhed by *Barksdale*, pag. 18, *and* 19. tells us, That *Moſes* his Books, wherein thoſe Miracles are recorded, which at the *Iſraelites* coming out of Ægypt, and in the wilderneſs, and in their entrance into the land of *Canaan* had happened, are of certain credit; not only becauſe the preſent *Jews* from their Parents, as they from theirs, and ſo forward until we arrive at thoſe who lived in *Moſes* and *Joſhua* his time, by certain and conſtant Tradition have received thoſe miracles, but also

also, because there hath been a perpetual fame among the *Hebrews*, that *Moses* was commended by the Oracle of God, and made a Leader of his People; and because it is sure enough, that he was neither studious of his own glory, nor partial to his own Posterity. All which declares, saith *Grotius*, he had no reason to deceive us. Now, finding this *Theology* of the *Chinois*, not by tradition, and a perpetual fame, but in Books successively written from Age to Age, ever since the universal Deluge, above seven hundred years before *Moses* was born, to be equally agreeable and consonant to what CHRIST himself and *Moses* hath taught us, and what we profess. And that in writing of these Books, the *Chinois* were neither studious of their own glory, nor partial to their own posterity, which declares they had no reason to deceive us. I see no cause to doubt, but that they received this *Their Theology*, *ex doctrina à Nöe tradita*, from the doctrine taught them by *Noah*, as *Martinius* from their Books hath positively affirmed. Considering withal, that *Noah was a just man, and perfect in his generations, and Noah walked with God.* Gen.6.v.9.

Isaack Chron.pag. 47.

As for Their policy in government, I shall chiefly observe what *Kircherus* delivers. That if ever any Monarchy in the world was constituted according to political principles, and dictates of right reason, it may be boldly said that of the *Chinois* is. For therein every thing is found disposed in so great order; as that whereas all matters are under the rule and power of their *Literati*, or wisemen; so also hardly any thing is transacted throughout the whole Empire which

A. Kirch. Chi. Ill. par. 2: p. 115

depends

depends not upon them; neither can any man
attain to any degree of Honour, that is not very
richly learned in their Letters and Sciences. In
a word, their Kings may be said to be Philosophers, and their Philosophers, Kings; and they
order every thing, faith *Semedo*, in such manner, *Al. Sem.*
as may most conduce to good government, con- *Rel. del.*
cord, peace, and quietness in families, and to the *Cin. par. 1.*
exercise of vertue: Insomuch he tels us, that so *cap. 18.*
great an Empire seemeth to be but, as it were,
one well governed Convent.

Their first form of Government, until the time
of their Emperours was paternal, as is written
of *Abraham* and *Lot*. But no credit is given to
whatever their History relates, during this form *M. Mart.*
of rule. For the *Chinois* themselves, as hath been *Sin. hist.*
said, suspect the credit of their Annals before the *lib. 1. pag. 12*
reign of their Emperour *Folmis*, as containing
those things, that are for the most part ridiculous
and false.

Their first Emperours were elective, but about
the year before CHRIST two thousand, two
hundred, and seaven, which according to the
Hebrew or vulgar computation, and which with
our *Chinique* Authors we follow, was forty four
yeares before the Confusion of Tongues, they
began to rule by hereditary right; and for numerous successions after the flood were not Idolaters, but Adorers of the true God of Heaven and
Earth; and were Priests also, and offered sacrifices to him; as no question from the Example
of *Noah* they had learned; and as the Patriarchs
Abraham, Isaac, and *Jacob* were afterwards accustomed to do. For, it was not lawful, faith

Martinius

Martinius, for any to officiate in *facris* but the Emperour; nor for any to be invested with the facerdotal dignity, but he that fwayed the fcepter, fo highly have they ever reverenced their facred matters. Neither was Idolatry known unto them, till after the birth of CHRIST, when for many Ages preceding, the whole World had followed Idols; for, the Offspring of *Cham* derive their Idolatry even from the time of *Noah*; and the *Ifraelites* themfelves had deferted God above one thoufand years before. But *Corruptio optimi peffima*, for after the *Chinois* fell into Idolatry, neither *Babylonians*, *Ægyptians*, or *Greeks* were ever more fuperftitious, nor ever had more Deities, than they.

Purch. Pilgrimage, lib. 1. pag. 67.

Cafting off their antient Theology, they entertained that error of the Eternity of the World; with which, as *Martinius* informeth us, together with the worfhip of Idols, they were, in the fixty fifth year after CHRIST, infected by an *Indian* Philofopher that crept into *China*, as *Xaverius* the Jefuit to propagate the Gofpel among them, did of late times. But as the *Jews* at this day hold it a fin to pronounce *Jehovah*; fo, their prefent Idolatry notwithftanding, the *Chinois* at this day hold it hainous for any, but their Emperour to facrifice to *Xangti*; infomuch that they put thofe to death that attempt the fame. But this their antient knowledg of, and conftant perfeverance in the worfhip of the true God requires as yet, a more ferious confideration; For we find in *Jofephus* that *Noah* at his coming forth of the Ark offered a facrifice of Thankfgiving unto God for his deliverance, but

M. Mart. Sin. Hift. lib. 1. p. 11.

Bayl. Pr. of piety. p. 19, 20.

M. Mart. Sin. Hift. lib. 1. p. 48.

Jof. Ant. Jud. lib. 1. cap. 4.

read

read nothing more of any such worship, till the dayes of *Abraham*; who we are taught, was by God himself peculiarly chosen, and called thereunto; *Gen.* 12. And who, saith the same *Josephus*, firſt of all did moſt manifeſtly preach and prove, that there was but one God, Governour and Maker of all things. When as in *China* one God, by whom all things are governed and preſerved, was not only adored, during all that time from *Noah* unto *Abraham*; but alſo hath continually from *Abraham* to this very day, been adored amongſt them; their *Literati* eſpecially. So that had this extreme part of *Asia* been diſcovered in the time of St. *Augustine*, he might have aſſigned far larger bounds to his City of God, and *the Tents of Sem*, than otherwiſe he hath done.

That which *Aristotle* hath delivered of the People of *Asia*, is verified in the nature of the *Chinois*: We *Europeans* exceed them in point of valour, They us in ſubtlety of invention. They are wiſe, politique, and upon ſuddain emergencies moſt acute and reſolute. Laborious alſo they are and induſtrious, and ſuffer not any one thing that is uſeful to be loſt. For notwithſtanding their great abundance of all precious commodities, they collect and keep together the moſt vileſt and baſeſt rags whatſoever, the bones of Dogs, Hens feathers, Hogs hairs, yea all ſorts of moſt filthy and ſtinking excrements, and make good merchandize of them. Their fineneſs of ingenuity is oftentimes perverted; for, they take great pleaſure to outwit, and craftily cozen others. But they are profeſſed enemies to ſloth and idleneſs, and where the leaſt hope of gain appears,

Id. cap.8.

M. Mart.
Atl. Sin.
p. 5.

Id. pag. 7. pears, they think no pains too great to obtain it. They are healthful and strong, very agile, nimble, and of a lively spirit, and in some places contend with *Europæans* for whiteness of complexion, and are much conformable to them, if the flat nose, thin beard, prominent and long eyes, and broad face be excepted. All both men and women delight in long and black hair on the head. The women generally are low of stature, but in countenance both generous and elegant. The chief grace and beauty of a woman they attribute to the smalness of her feet. Wherefore, as soon as they are born, they swaddle and bind them with fillets so streightly, that they can never after grow. Insomuch that some of them in bigness scarcesly exceed Goats or Calves-feet. A ridiculous verily and strange folly in such a polite people, to whom if an *Helena* were brought, they would arraign her of deformity if her feet were greater. So that their women endure willingly that kind of torment, that they may appear the more amiably pleasing to the men.

The first Arts of the *Chinois* were the Mathematiques, Astrology, and Astronomy, of which that they might receive the Elements from *Noah*, I conceive none will suspect, the progeny of *Seth* before the flood having made such progress therein, as that by writing they communicated M. Mart. Sin. hist. lib. 1. p. 17. to posterity what they had found out concerning them. *Inde constat scientiam primam apud Sinas Mathematicam fuisse, atque a Noe ad posteros quasi per manus propagatam* ; whereby it appears, saith *Martinius*, that the first science amongst the *Chinois* was the Mathematical, and from *Noah*

to

to their Posterity delivered as it were by hand.

They delight in no Art more, than Agricul- *Id. lib. 8.* ture and Planting, nor ever from all Antiquity *pag. 330.* did, and are to admiration expert therein. Insomuch that without prejudice to other Nations it may be affirmed truly, they exceed all people in the World, and are so indefatigably diligent, laborious and expert therein, that throughout all the *Chinique* Empire, there is scarcely one hands bredth of ground to be found unmanured or barren, that either by Nature is, or by Art can be made fertile. And therefore no wonder that such multitudes of people are fully supplied with all manner of Provisions: Nor that they should be so expert, since that *Noah* was an husbandman and taught them. The ninth part of the land is the Emperour's; for, upon settling any new Colony they always made an equal division, allotting to every family alike proportion, which they subdivided again into nine parts, whereof that in the middest was the Emperours. Whereby as the safety of the Emperour lay in the hearts of his Subjects, so his lands also lay in the heart of Theirs.

Their Physick consists in the knowledg of Plants and Herbs, of all other undoubtedly the most safe and secure, and most agreeable to the constitutions and complexions of Mankind. And they are so learned and expert herein, that they *M. Mart.* say one of their Emperours having in the space *Sin.hist.lib.* of one day found out sixty several sorts of poy- *1.p.24.* sonous simples, in the same day likewise found out, as many other Herbs, as were Antidotes

H   against

against them; whom therefore they call the Prince and Author of Physicians at this day. But our *Europæans* find their profit too easie by consulting *Galen*, to trouble themselves with so great study, as this kind of practice requires.

A. Kir. Ch. Ill. par. 4. p. 169.

Ours talk, *Theirs* cure, saith *Martinius*. Their Physicians, saith *Kircherus* also, being learned by Tradition (traditional practice, are his Authors, *Martinius* words) are famously skilful in the knowledg of Pulses, whereby the causes, effects, and symptoms of Diseases are admirably discovered by them, and agreeable remedies accordingly applied. They never write any receipt, but give the Medicine themselves unto the Patient whom they visit, and whom at their coming they never ask where his pain lieth, whether in his head, stomack, or belly, but feel his pulse only with both their hands leaning on a pillow, or some such other thing, and so observe the motion of it, for a good while, and from thence declare what the Patient aileth; the learned Physicians seldom failing therein.

A. Sem. Rel. de la Cin. par. 1. 6. 11.

Poetry is of high Antiquity amongst them. But it is far different from that, that is in use with us; For, they stuff not their works with Fables, Fictions, and Allegorical conceits, such as when the Authors Poetical rapture is over, himself understands not. But in *Heroick* verse chant forth instructions for their Princes to govern justly, their Ministers of State to rule under them uprightly; and their Subjects to obey them loyally: and in such manner composed withal; that they infuse terrour into the bad, and are a spur to the good to live vertuously and well. Other Poems they

M. Mart. Sin. hist. lib. 4. p. 111.

have

have which are the subject of Natural Philosophy; and others again, which treat of Love, not with so much levity nevertheless, as ours, but in such chaste Language, as not an undecent and offensive word to the most chaste ear is to be found in them. And which is more, they have no Letters whereby to express the *Privy parts*, nor are they to be found written in any part of all their Books; which cannot be said of any Language under the concave of Heaven, besides. Now, why may not this more than remarkable silence proceed, out of the detestation of that shame, which *Noah* received by the discovery of his nakedness, as a reproach throughout *Their* generations to be for ever buried in oblivion? And be the cause also, why Wine made of grapes should be odious to them? So that heretofore the Jesuites were enforced to have the wine which they used in their Ceremony of the Mass from *Macao* at exceeding charge, labour, and no less peril; lest, as it were, it should be discovered. But, now they procure it from *Xansi*, to administer in such Provinces, where otherwise it is not to be had. It is observable likewise, that he, who during the reign of *Iuus*, found out the way to make wine of Rice, was banished for his industry; and though severe punishments were by publique edict decreed against all those that either made or drank it, nevertheless from this kind of liquor they could never be induced to refrain; superstition might perswade them to despise the *One*; no Policy could compel them to forbear the *Other*.

As for Moral Philosophy, their Ancestors had these five Cardinal Vertues, *Piety, Justice, Policy,*

A Sem. Rel. de la Cin. par. 1. cap. 11.

M. Mart. Sin. hist. lib. 1. p. 54.

A. Sem. Rel. de la Cin. par. 1. cap. 29.

Piu-

Prudence, *Fidelity* in such high esteem, as that all their most antient and fundamental Laws were framed out of them, neither are they in less account amongst them at this day, than in times of old. We will take leave to repeat them, as they in their own Idiom express them, thus, *Gin, Y, Li, Chi, Sin.*

Gin, they say, signifies *Piety, Humanity, Chari-ty, Reverence, Love, Compassion*, which after this manner they explain, *To* esteem ones self less than others ; *To* be affable ; *To* succour those that are afflicted ; *To* help those that are in necessity ; *To* have a tender and compassionate heart; *To* bear good will towards all men ; *To* use all this more particularly towards their Parents.

Y, according to their doctrine is *Justice, Equality, Integrity, Condescention* in all things reasonable and just ; hereby the Judge is, *To* give every man his own. The rich man, *To* take heed he presume not on his wealth ; and *To* give some part of it to the Poor ; *To* adore, as *Martinius* hath it, the Supreme Emperour of Heaven and Earth ; *Not* to be contentious ; *Not* to be obstinate ; *Not* to oppose what is just, and conformable to reason.

Li, as they expound it, is *Policy, Courtesie*, to honour and reverence others as is fitting, which they say, consisteth, *In* the mutual respect one man is to bear another ; *In* the mature consideration and circumspection which is to be used in managing of affairs ; *In* the modesty of outward deportment ; *In* obedience to Magistrates; *In* being gentle to young men, and respectful to old.

Chi, after their Philosophy, denoteth *Prudence*

dence, *Wisedom* ; the which they place, *In* read-ing of Books, *In* studying of Sciences ; *In* being perfect in the liberal Arts ; *In* the knowledg of matters of Antiquity ; *In* the good intelligence of modern affairs ; *In* observing well what is past, thereby the better to regulate the present and future occasions ; *In* discerning right from wrong.

Sin, they say, is *Fidelity, Verity,* it consisteth in a sincere heart, and real intention ; *To* do only that which is good ; *To* imitate what is just ; *To* make their words and works, and that which is hidden within, to that which appeareth outwardly, agree.

As they have these five Cardinal qualities, so they reckon up five principal degrees of Humane Society, The *King* and *Subject* ; the *Husband* and *Wife* ; *Father* and *Son* ; *Elder* and *Younger Brothers* ; and one *Friend* to *Another*. The *King* is to observe towards his *Subjects, Love, Vigilancy,* and *Clemency* : and the *Subjects* towards the *King, Loyalty, Reverence,* and *Obedience.* The *Husband* towards his *Wife, Love, kind usage,* and *union* : *She* towards her *Husband, Fidelity, Respect,* and *Complacency.* The *Father* towards his *Children, Love* and *Compassion* ; They *toward* their *Father, Obedience* and *Piety.* The *Elder Brother* towards the *Younger, Love,* and *Instruction* ; The *Younger* towards the *Elder* , (that is, to all their *Brothers* that are *Elder* than they) *Observance* and *Respect.* *Friends* towards one *Another, Love, Faithfulness,* and *Sincerity.* And as for degrees of lesser ranck *M. Mart.* appertaining to visits, entertainment of guests, *Sin. Hist.* civil and modest behaviour, and what belongeth *lib. 4. p. 146*

to

to the decent compofure of the body, they enu-
merate no lefs, than three thoufand, of all which
in their Books, they treat moft largely.

And for better propagation of Learning their
Emperours erected *Publique Schools*, and *Acade-
mies*, that their Subjects might be inftructed, in
whatever Arts and Moral Vertues; whereby
from their childhood growing up to the elegancy of moft excellent abilities; they were indued
with obfervance to their Elders, and duty towards their Parents; who with all the moft fub-
miflive reverence, were ever; and ftill are honou-
red by them, not only during their lives, but after death likewife; fo that no People under the
Sun with more regret, and greater ceremony
condole the lofs of their Parents, than the *Chinois*; Never for three years together after their
deaths, ftirring out of their doors; never fitting in
a chair, but on a little ftool; never lying on a bed-
ftead, but the floor; never drinking any of their
wine; eating flefh, ufing any baths; or, if you
will believe them, lying with their wives; nor
ever, during that time tranfacting any publique
Affairs, whatever Office of State they are entruft-
ed with; even from the Emperour to the meaneft degree of Magiftrates. This being done by
them, faith *Martinius*, that from the refpect which
the living give unto the dead, their children
may learn in what manner living Parents are to
be refpected. As if their firft Founder had taught
them, *Honour thy father and thy mother, that thy
days may be long upon the land, which thy Lord thy
God giveth thee.* Exod. 20. v. 12. And certain it is,
that throughout their whole Empire, they are
                                                   generally

*A. Sem.
Rel. de la
Cin. par. 1.
cap. 16.*

*M. Mart.
hiſt. Sin.
lib. 9. pag.
378.*

generally known to live a long and happy life. We read, that there have been those amongst them, whose bones were twelve or thirteen Cubits long, and that they lived one thousand years and more; which if so, it must be before the flood. But in regard this seems to spring from Tradition only, if according to *Nieuhoff* it be looked upon as a vapour of the *Chinois*, and that with him we admit it into the rank of Fables, yet the reason that he gives for its untruth, doth not hold good against it. For, he saith, the Holy Scripture tells us, that not one of the men of the first Age of the World lived unto a thousand years. Now that there were Giants both before and after the flood is manifest, *Gen.* 6. *v.* 4. *Deut.* 3. *v.* 11. And though we find *Methusalah* to have lived nine hundred sixty nine years; nevertheless, that he was the longest liver of all the men of the first Age of the World, we need not grant, neither is he by *Moses* precisely so recorded to be. Indeed as to those ten generations, that from the Creation to the Deluge, proceeded from *Adam*, by the line of *Seth*, with their several Ages, we must acknowledge it to be true, but whether those seven of the line of *Cain*, or any of their Progeny outlived any of those of the other ten, is not expressed in Sacred story. And it will seem more probable, saith Dr. *Brown*, "That of the "line of *Cain*, some were longer liv'd than any "of *Seth*, if we concede that seven genera-"tions of the cne, lived as long as nine of the other. That *Adam*, who never was so young as any, was older than all, is conceived by learned men. "And if the usual compute will hold, that men

A.Sem.Rel. de la Cin. par.l.cap.1

J.Nieuh. Amb.Or. par.1. pag.122.

Dr.Bro. Pseudod. Epid.lib.8. pag.255.

H 4 are

" are of the same Age which are born within
" the same year, *Eve* was as old as her husband
" and Parent *Adam*, and *Cain* their son coeta-
" neous to both. However, certain it is, that the
Chinois, in vigour and perfect health, live commonly unto seventy, eighty or an hundred years
of Age.

The loss of Parents amongst them is not so
much condoled by their children, but that children are as dear unto their Parents, from whence
it proceeds, that their Nobility are so averly dif-
posed that the Emperour should marry any of
their daughters, because when once setting foot
within his Palace, they are eternally deprived of
N.Trig. in Christ. Exp. apud Sin. lib. 1. p. 83. their sig't. Hence, if beautiful, they conceal them
from publique view, left more than ordinary no-
tice should be taken of them, and information
given accordingly to the Court. And hence, the
Emperours wife comes generally to be of the
meanest of the people, not her extract, but
beauty being respected. And it is a Maxime with
their *Literati*, that to deprive a father of his child,
is to take away a beam from the Sun, the source
from the Fountain, the member from the body,
and the branch from the tree. Thus, for father-
ly affection and filial piety, *China* may give example to all Nations of the World. The union
is reciprocal ; the Parents indulge their children, and the children esteem no time more unfortunate, than that same hour, which gives beginning to the fatal period of their Parents
lives.

In their Marriages they seem to have much
Analogy with the *Hebrews*. For as in the Law
of

of *Moſes,* Levit. 18. *Theſe* were prohibited to marry within certain degrees of conſanguinity; ſo, by the Laws of their Foreſathers, our *Chinois* were not to wed any of the ſame name, which to this day they obſerve: Again, as the *Chinois* have been accuſtomed to have two ſorts of wives; a matrimonially wedded wife, and a Concubine, both of them accounted lawful; ſo, the *Hebrews* had two ſorts of wives, a wife married with nupⸯ tial ceremonies, and a Concubine, both of them reputed lawful. As the wife of *Theſe* was as Miſtreſs, and the Concubine as an hand-maid or ſervant; ſo, the Concubine of *Thoſe* was in ſubⸯ jection to the true wife, and as a ſervant upon ſeveral occaſions ſerved her. Alſo the children by both wives were held legitimate in either Nation. As likewiſe when the Concubine had brought forth a ſon, the wife might, if ſhe pleaſed ſend her away, as *Sarah* did *Hagar*, Gen. 21. v. 10. But in *China*, where all theſe rituals are ſtill obſerved, the Child ſtays behind, acknowledging only for his mother, his fathers lawful wife.

A. Sem.
Rel. de la
Cin. par. 1.
cap. 15.
T. Godwin
Ant. Jud.
lib. 6. cap. 4

The Widows of the *Chinique* Gentry are generally inacceſſable to a ſecond marriage. And their Virgins that by an untimely death have loſt their Lovers, forſaking all worldly pleaſures retire commonly into the deſart mountains, leading in them a moſt deplorable and lamentable life, never by any allurements of their Parents or Friends to be reclaimed, until either Lions or Tigers intomb them in their bowels. But although as well their Virgins, as Widows are thus chaſtly reſolved. Barrenneſs in wedlock nevertheleſs,

nevertheless, is, by them as with the *Hebrews*
placed in the number of their chiefest calamities, not only by their Kings and Rulers, but also by the meanest of the people. And to be enforced to depart, with the inheritance belonging
to their Ancestors, is, they conceive the greatest
misery that can befal them.

We read of *Solomon*, that he prayed to God, to
give him an understanding heart. 1 *Reg.* 3. *v.* 9.
How nearly the First and Antient Emperours of
China may example this, let their History declare:
For, being now upon their marriages, I shall only instance the prayer of a *Chinois* imploring a
blessing upon his. In the Province of *Honan*, saith
Martinius, one called *Tetriang* being to be married, is thus reported to have invoked Heaven: *I
require not Riches, nor Pleasures; neither therefore
would I take a wife, but pray for good children only.*
And by his wife he had three sons, which all pro-
ved most learned Philosophers, and just Governours. His memory remaineth not only in their
Annals, but by a stately monument erected to his
honour.

As for interrment of their dead, the *Chinois*
have always used to bury every one in the place
of the sepulture of his Progenitors, be it never
so remote from that Territory where he dies;
which happeneth oftentimes to their Rulers,
who being not to be advanced to the Government of any place, within that Province where
they were born, are sent to command in several
other parts of the Empire; and therby many times
departing this life out of their own Countrey,
are upon that occasion brought home, and buried

M. Mart.
Atl. Sin.
p. 62.

A. Sem.
Rel. de la
Cin. par. 1.
cap. 16.

ied therein. As the body of *Jacob* was translated out of *Ægypt* upon the same account, *Gen.* 50. *v.* 7. and buried in the same sepulcher, wherein these five *Abraham, Isaac, Sarah, Rebekah,* and *Leah* were laid, himself making the sixth; the first Letters of all their names being contained in, hat one name of ISRAEL. so likewise were the bones of *Joseph* carried up out of *Ægypt,* and inhumed in *Sychem* in the land of *Canaan,* Exo. 13. *v.* 19. where in like manner the other Patriarchs were buried, *Act.* 7. *v.* 16. And even by the modern *Jews* this custome is observed at this day from a conceited opinion; ; "That if an " *Israelite* be buried in any strange Countrey out " of the promised land, he shall not be partaker " so much as of the Resurrection, except the " Lord vouchsafe to make him *hollow passages* un- " der the earth, through which his body by a con- " tinual volutation and rolling may be brought " into the land of *Canaan.* Wherefore from *Italy,* and other places where they are tolerated, I have heard, that oftentimes they fraight whole Ships with coffins of dead bodies, which are transported to the Ports of *Syria,* and thence conveyed into *Judæa,* and there interred.

T. Godwin Ant. Jud. lib. 6. c. 5.

Furthermore, the *Chinois* observe the New and Full Moon-days with great ceremony, and reckon the year by the Moon like the *Hebrews,* nearly relating to whom, they have many more observances and institutions customary with them. Amongst others the like Commandments, which they print, and set up on the posts of their doors towards the street; *As not to kill; not to steal; not to lie; to honour Father and Mother,* &c. *Semedo*

A. Sem. Rel. de la Cin. par. 1. cap. 29.

indeed

indeed thinks these not antient, but that from all Antiquity, till their falling into Idolatry, they were not to make the resemblance of any thing in point of adoration, *Martinius* hath fully assured us. And how antient soever the rest be, upon every day of the New and Full Moon, a little before Sun-rising, at one and the same hour, they make solemn publication of them, in all the Cities, and all the streets throughout their whole Empire.

M. Mart.
Ail. Sin.
P. 71.

In the Province of *Suchuen* the same *Martinius* relates a memorable thing to have hapned. For they write, saith he, that a certain woman, walking by the side of the river *Chocung*, which runs by the City of *Kiating*, perceived a reed in the water, from whence a voice proceeded, and taking it up found an infant lying therein (for the reeds or Canes in *China* are about the bigness of little vessels) which she carried home and brought up, and which not long after was called *Yelang*, and in those parts that tend into the West, gave beginning to the Kingdom of *Yelang*. And was not *Moses* found after the same manner in an Ark of bulrushes, taken up and educated by the daughter of *Pharoah*? And what an high Princedome he afterwards attained, we all know.

What should I say of the conversation of the *Chinois*? It inchants their familiars rather, than delights them. What of their Entertainments? They are stately and magnificent, and performed so silently, and in such goodly order, as is not by any pen to be expressed. What of the education of their Children? It makes all those admire that see them, being not brought up to wantonness

ness of speech, oftentation in habits, alluring enticements, to liberty and pleafures; but unto duties befeeming their fex and condition; not knowing what either arrogancy or impudency means. So that their daughters not bring portions to their husbands; but their Husbands provide all things whatfoever that are needful for them. What of their fervants? When every one, even the meaneft, with due refpect and awful filence, knows how to do, and doth it. What of the difpofition of their Natures generally? Since, enjoying all kind of the moft wealthy commodities, by which they might infinitely enrich themfelves, they fell them at inconfiderable prizes, defiring food and raiment only, as *Jacob* did, Gen. 28. v. 20.

We might acquiefce here, and now infift no longer on particulars, thefe being fufficient to declare, that *China* is the moft antient, and in all probability, was, the firft planted Countrey of the World after the flood. But in regard it is much to be prefumed that as wel *Afia* as *Europe* is extremely indebted to this induftrious Nation; from which as from the fountain they have drained all their chiefeft Arts and Manufactures, fomwhat more of their ingenuity is yet remaining to be faid. For the *Chinois* invented and have had in ufe amongft them, the Loadftone and compafs for Navigation, above eleven hundred years before the birth of CHRIST. An undoubted argument that the ufe thereof being fo long time fince found out by the *Chinois*, hath from them in mine opinion, faith *Martinius*, been brought into other Countreys.

M. Mart.
Sin. Hift.
lib. 4. p. 106

The

Id.lib.8.
Pag.334.

The making of paper the best undoubtedly of the World, was invented by them, above an hundred and eighty yeares preceding CHRIST, before which time they used the barques and leaves of trees; and until they had invented ink, with a bodkin or stile of iron dextrously formed their Letters. They writ also many things on Lamins or plates of mettal, and also on vessels of molten mettal, of which there are some yet remaining, which are held in no small esteem by the owners, and all that see them. But now they use paper, which is of so many sorts, and in so great abundance, that I am perswaded, saith *Semedo*, *China* in this exceedeth the whole universe; and is exceeded by none in the goodness thereof.

A.Sem.
Rel.de la
Cin.pa.1.
cap.6.

M.Mart.
Atl.Sin.
p.107.

The making of Ink is amongst their *Literati* a liberal Art, as all things else that appertain to learning; and it is made by them of the smoke of oyle, after the same manner possibly, as we do washing colour of the smoke of wood; and being not liquid but solid, they prepare it much after the like way, as our Painters do colours; for they grind it on a smooth stone, dissolve it in water, and then use it, not with a pen but pensil made of the flocks of an Hare, so that whereas antiently, (as was remembred) they writ with a style of iron, they may now in regard of their pensil be said to paint rather, than write their Characters. This Ink is usually brought into *Europe*, and the Letters, which we see, formed thereon, (for it is cast out of an oblong or parallelogram mould,) are verses in praise thereof, the workmans name being added.

The Art of Printing which had its original

among

among them about the fiftieth yeare after CHRIST, we owe unto their studies alfo. Their manner is thus, they cut their Letters with an inftrument of iron, as we do woodprints, upon a piece of Pear-tree, or fome fuch other fmooth wood, lightly gluing the written copy thereon, whereby their books are free from all Errata's. They are very dextrous at it, and will cut an whole fheet, as foon as a Compofer with us can fet one, and one man will print off fifteen hundred in a day. This commodity they have alfo, that they may be laid by for as many impreffions as they pleafe, and in the mean time print off, no more copies, than they find fale for, both which advantages are wanting in our manner of Printing.

M. Mart. Sin. Hift. lib. 8. p. 353.

One of their Emperours by the means of Chymiftry, found out that thrifty and frugal way of killing of men, by the invention of Guns and Gunpowder. But the time when, I find not in any Author. Their ftore of Powder is very great; in the ufe of their Guns they have little skill and lefs delight; but in making Fire-works are moft curioufly artificial, reprefenting Trees, Fruits, Battles; with what not other rarities. About which at the folemnity of the New year, we have feen, faith *Trigantius*, at *Hanking* more Powder fpent in one moneth, than for two years would ferve for continual War.

J. Nieuh. l' Amb. Or. par. 2. pag. 30.

N. Trig. in Chi. Exp. apud Sin. lib. 1. p. 18.

The Manufacture alfo, of making and dying of Silk was invented and taught unto women by the wife of their Emperour *Jaus*. And it is an honour to the *Chinois*, and worthy their reputation, faith *Martinius*, that, that kind of Manufacture,

M. Mart.
Sin. Hist.
Lib. 1. p. 38 facture, as from the original spring, was, into *Asia* and *Europe* derived and brought from *China.*

I had almost forgotten their Potters mystery, the manner of their making of *Porcelain* dishes, cups, vases, and the like utensils; which the richest Cabinets of the greatest Princes not of *Europe* and *Asia* only, but throughout the whole World also, glory to enjoy; and for which the *Chinois* are most singularly famous. It is indeed, saith *Semedo*, the sole vessel in the Universe for neat and delightful cleanliness; and therefore A. Sem.
Rel. de la
Cin. par. 1.
cap. 4. the *Chinois* reject to be served in plate, there being scarcely to be found amongst them, no not so much as in the Emperours Palace, a vessel of silver of any considerable bigness, but generally all they use are *Porcelain.*

It hath been commonly reported, that they make their *Porcelain* of Egg-shells, or the shells of Sea-fish beaten to powder, which they cast up in an heap within the bowels of the Earth, and therein let it lie an hundred years at least, before the matter will be ripe for making of those utensils. Which many ages even to this present have vulgarly received for a truth, hath nevertheless by learned men been much suspected alwayes, and now, the same may be worthily laughed at.

J. Nieuh.
l'Amb. Or.
par. 1. pag.
117. The *Porcelain* then of the best sort is made at a place called *Sinktesim* in the Province of *Kiang-si,* and in other Towns thereof likewise but not so good; the principal Magazine or Mart of it, and from whence it is dispersed throughout all *China,* is the Town of *Urienien* within the same Province,

Province, being diſtant from *Sinkleſimo* about forty leagues. It ſeems very ſtrange, that in all the precinᶜts of *Kiangſi* there cannot any earth be found proper to make the ſame, but they are enforced to fetch it from the Province of *Nanking*, not far from the City of *Hoeicheu*, where neither can they make it, which ſeems no leſs ſtrange, though there the material abounds. Some attribute the cauſe thereof to the quality of the water, others to the quality of the wood, or temperature of the fire. But whatſoever it be, certain it is, that the Earth, whereof they make their *Porcelain*, is taken out of the mountains of *Hoang*, that environ the ſaid City of *Hoeicheu*, where they form it into ſquare lumps, of the weight of three *Catteos* [which make about four pounds of our weight, allowing ſixteen ounces to the pound] and in value half a *Condrin* [or fifteen pence ſterling] which are tranſported to *Sinkleſimo*, and thoſe other places they make it at, by ordinary Mariners; who for avoiding all ſuch deceits, as are commonly incident to the carriage and ſelling of Comodities and Merchandize, are obliged to take an Oath not to imbezil any, at leaſt thoſe, that are marked with the Emperours Arms. As to the nature of the Earth it is very meager or lean, but fine and ſhining like Sables, which they temper in water to reduce it into the faſhion of thoſe little ſquare lumps. When likewiſe at any time the *Porcelain* breaks, they ſtamp and pound the broken pieces, and again make other utenſils thereof, which nevertheleſs have nothing of the luſtre, brightneſs and beauty of the former. They prepare the earth

I   and

and fashion it almost after the same manner, as the *Italians* do, for making of their dishes at *Faenza*, or, as the *Hollanders* for their white Potters-work. The *Chinois* are extremely quick and agile in giving perfection to these vessels, and very expert in enriching them with glorious colours, diaphanous and transparent. They represent upon them all sorts of Animals, Flowers, and Plants, with an inimitable grace and propriety. They are so jealous also of this their Science, that one may sooner draw Oyl out of an Anvile, than the least secret of it from their mouths. Infomuch, that he passeth amongst them for one of the greatest Criminals, that reveals this Art to any, but his own children. They make use of *Indigo* or *Woad* (which groweth abundantly in the Southern Provinces of the Empire) when with blew they would paint their work. They are said likewise, to prepare their earth different ways; and that some make vessels of it, as they receive the same, and as it comes first to hand; and that some again quite contrary dry it, until it be as hard as a flint, then beat and pound it in mortars or mills, which done they searce it, and with water knead it like like dough, and thereof form their vessels, into what figure they please; which for a long time they expose to the winds and Sun, before they bring them to the Fire. Now, when they are throughly dried they put them into * furnaces of timber well stopped, whereto for fifteen days together they keep continual fire, which expired, they also let them stand therein as many days more, to the end they may cool gently, and

be

* *Four-*
neau x à
voit bien
vou hes.

Be lefs apt to break ; for experience hath taught
them, that when they take them hot out of the
fire, they break like glafs. The fire muſt be made
of very dry and light wood , otherwiſe the
ſmoke blackens, and renders them cloudy, and
dulls the nobleneſs of their gloſs , which is not
made or proceeds but from a ſtrong, equal and
proportionable heat. The thirty days being paſt,
the Superintendent of this myſtery comes to o-
pen the furnaces, and after having viewed thoſe
that are made ; takes by way of Tribute the fifth
part for the Emperour , according to the Law
eſtabliſhed in the Country.

But whatſoever elſe in relation to their induſtry, we have remembred, or omitted their ingenuity in making of floating Iſlands , is not in
ſilence to be buried. The ſtructure of which is
ſo graceful and natural , as that one would imagine them to be Iſlands indeed. Theſe moving
Machines are made of thoſe reeds, which the
Portugals call *Bamboes* , and which are bound together unto little joyſts with cords, but ſo arti-
ficially and neatly, that no moiſture can ever of-
fend the inhabitants, who dwell in Cabbins built
and raiſed upon the ſame. All which are made
of planks, matts, and ſuch other light materials,
and their ſtreets are ſo well ordred , that one
would conceive them to be little Villages , and
ſome are ſo great, that they contain two hundred
families. Upon theſe they commodiouſly tranſport their Wares and Merchandizes, and ſell them
to thoſe which live upon the banks of the River
Crocens. And for removing of them, they uſe
no Sails , but either by ſtrength of arm tow

J. Nieuh.
l'Amb. Or.
p.ir.1,
pag.154.

them

them, or let them drive with the water, to the place where they intend to traffique ; where when arrived, they fix great stakes into the River, to which they fasten their Islands, during the time of their riding there,

Much might be said of their Architecture; for Palaces and Publique works especially, which are stupendious and prodigious rather, than magnificent and great. But being a particular discourse is more requisite for this, we shall forbear, and at present, from giving any other account thereof, desist.

That the Descendents of *Cham* were great Masters in the knowledg of Arts and Sciences, is not to be denied. For we read, That *Moses was learned in all the wisdom of the Ægyptians.* Act.7.v.22. Which being spoken for his praise, and by way of *Emphasis*, argueth the learning of that People to be very great. Now, though much cannot be said in what particulars their wisedom did really consist; yet what manner of Learning the *Chinois* certainly had, as much at least as conduceth to our purpose, you have briefly heard; That their knowledg in Divine matters, of the true God especially, was taught them by *Noah*, *Martinius* hath positively assured us, there is no doubt to be made. And we may almost boldly say, that the circumstances are so many, and of such weight, for *Noah's* living both before and after the flood in *China*; that more, and more valid cannot be produced to make good, *si sacra excipias*, any assertion of whatever kind. But how great soever the consequence thereof is, to make our Essay probable; Arguments

ments of no lefs validity, together with the confent of Authors have made appear, that *China* was peopled ere *Nimrod* and his Troops undertook the work for building of the Tower of *Babel*, and before the *Confufion of Tongues* hapned. Wherefore having thereby, according to the Scripture fixed the PRIMITIVE Language in *China* ; let us in the next place enquire, whether this Language may, by the *Commerce* and *Intercourfe*, which the *Chinois* have had with other Nations, be altered ; or by the *Conquefts* they have undergone, forgotten utterly and extirpated.

BUT firft it will not be impertinent, to let you know, the manner obferved by their Anceftors of old, for the peopling and enlarging of their Dominions, whereby what enfueth will the more clearly be underftood ; and whereby they will be found not as the Off-fprings of *Cham* and *Japhet*, through the greedy thirft of prey, cruel defire of revenge, and facred ambition of rule, to have ufually invaded their confining neighbours. But by juft and peaceable plantations, to have fetled themfelves throughout the now *China*. For, as *Martinius* faith, It is not to be imagined, that in thofe times their Empire extended over all *China*, as now; for it fcarcely comprehended as then, an indifferent part of the prefent Magnitude. For, as the firft Planters thereof coming from the Weft, began to inhabit the Province of *Xenfi*, in that part which lieth moft towards the Weft, fo the heads of their feveral families by degrees fought out new feats from thence. For, after the Province of *Xenfi*,

M. Mart.
Sin. Hift.
lib.4. p.
134.

I 3   the

the next *Hanan, Peking, Xantung* began to be inhabited. Which Provinces Imperial Dominion being thence forward eftablifhed among the *Chinois*, were all governed by a fingle perfon. The form of the Government was juft all the Provinces which lay alongft the great river of *Kiang* towards the North, acknowledging one Emperour, and to his Authority and rule of their own voluntary accord fubjecting themfelves.

But under *Yuus*, who was the third in fucceffion from *Jaus*, and who brought the Empire to an hereditary Dominion; all thofe Countries alfo, that lie on the South of that River were furveyed, and Geographical defcriptions made of them. The people of them neverthelefs were as yet but few, and fubmitted not to the fetled Monarchy of *China*. But afterwards when the Emperours had oftentimes many fons, excepting him that was Heir apparent, and to fucceed; the reft were either created Royallets of fome particular Territory, or elfe, by now and then leading forth of Colonies, fought out new habitations, and planted thofe Southern parts. After this manner then fetting up new Kingdoms, the people being delighted with the vertue of their Princes, their inventing, inftituting, and encouraging humane Arts, Husbandry efpecially, and others of the like kind, readily obeyed. Thus by degrees all *China*, farr and wide, in every part, as now, became to be inhabited; and as it was out of one body and one Off-fpring peopled, fo at length it grew into one body and form of Empire.

Having throughly fetled themfelves at home, their

their numbers multiplying, they began to look abroad, and after their usual custome by sending forth of Colonies planted the Peninsula of *Corea*, with the Island of *Japan*, which glories of her descent from them; so *Java*, *Ceilan*, or, as *Martinius* observes, *Sinlan* rather, because first peopled by the *Chinois*. As also the Island of St. *Laurence*, of which there can be no more assured testimony, than that it is still possessed by the *Chinois*, especially in the road of St. *Clara*; where the Inhabitants are white people, and at this very day speak the *Chinique* Tongue; as to the Sea-men putting in to that harbour is well known. And not only these, but likewise most of the Oriental Islands are of their Plantation. For, having Shipping, and the use of the Compass, whither might they not transport themselves? | *M. Mart: Sin. hist. lib.6.pag. 236.*

In the Continent likewise, that *Siam*, *Camboya*, and the adjacent Regions drew their original from the *Chinois* is evident. From whence it proceeds that they use the *Chinique* Letters, yea, and express the denominations of numbers, not by Figures but Characters, as the *Chinois* do.

And I could almost be apt no longer to admire at the stately Structures of *Mexico*; or how *Cusco* came to be such a regular City; nor wonder at the ingenuity, magnificence and government of those people, seeing *Martinius* is disposed to conceive, that from *China* they had their beginning also. I could be of opinion, saith he, that beyond *Corea* having with their Ships penetrated the Straits of *Anian* likewise, the *Chinois* frequented *America*, that part especially which lieth *Id. lib.8. pag.358.*

I 4

lieth towards the Weſt. And that, that people happily had their original from them: For their complexion, the manner of wearing their hair, and the Air of their faces, maketh it very probable to me, of certainty neverthelefs I can ſay nothing thereof.

　　But *G. Hondius* in his original of the *Americans* is confident of it, and by many rational arguments very probably proves the ſame. For, as he ſaith, it muſt of neceſſity be, that ſuch well ordred manner of living, Arts, Buildings, Policy, Writing, Books, great induſtry and inclination to all kind of learning, as amongſt thoſe of *Peru* and *Mexico* may be obſerved was derived from a more polite people than thoſe, by whom the reſt of *America* was planted. Which polite people are aſſerted by him to be the *Chinois*. Now, in regard my diſcourſe tends to another end, I ſhall unto what *Hondius* hath learnedly pleaded for them, in relation to thoſe of *Mexico*, add only, that their publique minds, manner of Oratory, with their grave, ſuccinct, and wiſe ſayings, do in great likelihood confirm them to be originally extracted from *China.* The Architecture of the *Mexicans*, as alſo of the *Peruvians*, is by him much inſiſted upon; becauſe for the ſtupendiouſneſs and vaſt dimenſions of the ſtones it equally correſponds with the works of *China,* whereunto I ſhall likewiſe ſay, that whereas the ornaments of the Temple at *Mexico*, than which a more ſtately was ſcarcely ever ſeen, conſiſted chiefly of Dragons and Serpents, variouſly and with much ingenuity compoſed; it is manifeſt, that the Pagods and Regal Palaces in *China*, are all

G. Hond. de Or. Amer. lib. 4. p. 223

all with the fame fort of enrichments, and in the
fame order generally adorned ; the Dragon being the Standard Royal of the *Chinique* Empire.
That fuch like ornaments in buildings were ufed
by other people , either in the Eaft or elfewhere,
I have not read in any Author, which hath oftentimes made me very folicitous from whence
the *Mexicans* fhould have them,they being graceful, great and noble, but I could never find it
out, until the late hiftories of the *Chinois* came
to my perufal , which have clearly fatisfied me,
that the manner of them is peculiarly proper to
China, was brought from thence, and in memory
and for the honour of that Monarchy continued
by the *Mexicans*.

As for *Peru* , whereas *Hondius* will have it to
be peopled by the *Chinois* , tranfported thither
under the conduct of *Mango* the firft of the *In-*
gas about four hundred years fince, I conceive,
they had difcovered it, and therein fetled themfelves divers Ages before. For, although *Mango*
with his followers might at that time to avoid
the fury of a prevailing Enemy forfake his native
Countrey, and landing in *Peru* , erect that Empire; neverthelefs confidering,that the *Spaniards*
at their entrance, found the maffive monuments
there, to bear fuch a decayed *Afpect*, as that they
demonftrated a far higher Antiquity, than the
date affigned ; and that it was ever cuftomary
with the *Chinois*, to fend forth the furplufage of
their numbers to fhift for themfelves , and feek
out new habitations ; fuch caftlings might in
their waudring throughout the South Sea (moft
of the Oriental Iflands being formerly inhabited
by

by their Off-spring) fall with the coaft of *Peru,* and finding it rich and delightful, poffefs themfelves thereof, and fettle there, until *Mango* with his company arrived, & united them all under his own Sovereignty, as *Hondius* hath delivered. The rather, in regard that after their native Country was cleared of that prevailing Enemy, which moft Writers, though erronioufly call the *Cathayans,* of whom, ere long, the *Chinois* voluntarily freed all the Iflands, and all their forein Plantations from obedience to them, and refted contented with thofe bounds, which God and Nature had primitively beftowed on them. And herein their contempt of vain glory is very obfervable, for how powerful foever they are, were, or might have been, if thirft of Dominion had provoked them, I never yet heard any of them all boaft of the extent or greatnefs of their Empire, faith *Trigantius.* And this now brings us to their War.

N. Trig. de Chrift. Exp. apud Sin. lib. 1. p. 59.

M. Mart. Sin. hift. lib. 1. p. 25.

The firft War ever read of in the World was made in *China,* happening in the Province of *Peking,* where, on the mountain *Fan,* near the City now called *Tenking,* their Emperour *Xinnungus* the Succeffor of *Fohius,* was, they fay, flain about the year before the birth of CHRIST two thoufand, fix hundred, ninety feven; which according to the Vulgar computation makes it before the flood about four hundred years. It was civil, and of this kind I find many, and moft bloody contefts to have been amongft them; but managed with fuch Heroick valour, and ftratagemical policy, as far furmounts all *Macedonian, Punique,* or any other known conduct in the World. Thefe Wars proceeded principally from the

the afpiring minds of the Royalets in the Southern Plantations, who were oftentimes many in
one and the fame Province, and ruled abfolutely
under the Sovereign, as fo many petty Kings;
though they paid Homage and Fealty to him,
much according to the fame manner, as Dukes and
Earls do, for the eftates they hold of the Emperours and Kings in *Europe.*

But after they were by little & little encreafed
in power, *fumptis in affines armis* taking up arms
againft their own kinred and affinity, they
troubled the whole Empire; out of Ambition
chiefly to reduce the Province in which they
governed, and were at firft fetled, under the
immediate command of themfelves, and their
own iffue without dependance upon a fuperiour.
And fometimes moreover attempting to ufurp
upon the Monarchy it felf; when either they
found their Sovereign was but weak in Councel,
or had dif-obliged his people; till in the end
they were all brought under abfolute fubjection
to the Monarch, and their Countries annexed to
the Imperial Crown, as they are at this day

But fuch civil difputes, you will happily fay,
could caufe no change of Language, no more
than the like contefts did between *Judah* and
Ifrael, being they were inteftine, and made a-
mongft the Natives themfelves of one Linage,
and the fame fpeech. For, it is not to be found
that ever foreign forces, were by any the moft
ambitious of all Royalets called in, or when
worfted invited to affift them with their Aides.
And thus the *Irifh* Tongue notwithftauding the
Domeftique wars, that almoft perpetually fucceeded

M. Mars.
Sin. hiff.
lib.6. pag.
243.

ceeded between the several Kings of that Island,
in the times of old, and notwithstanding *Danes*,
Norvegians, and *Scots* were frequently waged by
them to oppose the prevailing party, remained
uncorrupted, and so continueth at this present
time. Now, though these examples, and several
others of the like kind, may dictate to our reason,
hat by such wars, as these, their speech could not
be altered; nevertheless I must say, that you will
find, what through their long continuance,
sometimes without intermission for three hundred years together, what through the living
of the people without restraint in the mean
while, and becoming by Degrees thereby as rude
and barbarous, as the Regions they inhabited
were rough and mountainous, these civil discords
in *China*, did produce some difference in the
Language of these Provinces, where the greatest
fury of the war fell. But what this difference is,
and in what Provinces it doth differ, and in
which without change or alteration it remains
pure and perfect, we shall in its proper place,
not forget, particularly to remember.

Heylin affirmeth, that it is not lawful for the
King of *China* to make any war but meerly De-
fensive; and so, saith he, they enjoy a perpetual
peace. For, in regard war is equally destructive
to the victors and vanquished, Princes, People,
Treasure being alwayes consumed thereby; the
Chinois are of opinion, That nothing is more
unworthy their Emperour, than to enter into
armes unconstrained; nothing more inglorious,
than to seek for glory in the slaughter of his
subjects; nor more inhumane, than men by men

Heyl. Cosm.
Pag. 886.

to

o be cut in pieces. And hence without doubt it s, *Trigantius* tells us, that although he searched diligently into their Annals, from four thousand years unto his time to inform himself what forein conquests had been made by them, yet he could never find mention made of any : and that though oftentimes also, he seriously difcourfed with divers of their *Literati* about them, they all refolved him, that they never made, nor ever had been inclined to make any fuch. And therefore we are not to wonder, that we hear fo little of their invafions ; For, the wars excepted, which *Martinius* by a more full and free liberty of ftudy, hath of late found out to have been undertaken by their Emperours *Chingus* and *Hiarouus* their Hiftory, as to fuch expeditions, appears to be very filent.

N. *Trig. de Chrift. Exp. apud* Sin. *lib.* 1. *p.* 59.

Chingus firnamed *Xius* was the firft that by general confent was declared fupreme Monarch of all *China* ; and the firft Emperour of the Family of *Cina* ; from whence *Martinius* conceives the name *China* originally proceeded. This Prince having compelled feveral *Royalets* of the fouthern Provinces to fubmit wholly to his obedience, and thereby wonderfully enlarged the *Chinique* Empire ; extended his arms into remote parts, and both by fea and land over-ran all *India*, as far as *Bengala*, *Scori*, and *Camboya*. At which time being about two hundred and forty years before CHRIST the name and fame of the *Chinois* firft became known unto forein Nations, to their adjoining neighbours the *Indians* efpecially ; among whom it afterwards ftuck, and from them the *Portugals* at

their

their atchievements in *India* gained intelligence
of *China*. He made war upon the *Tartars* likewise, and by his victories in a short time enforced
them to abandon their habitations, and fly into
the more remote Regions of the North for
safety.

Id. pag. 238
A. Kirch.
Ch. Ill. par.
5. pag. 217. And this *Chingus* it was, that to secure his
Empire from the eruptions of that people; e-
rected that stupendious and wonderful work of
the wall touched on before. This wall beginning
at the sea-coast in *Leotung*, extendeth through
China unto *Lyncao* a City of *Xenfi*, seited on the
banks of the river *Croceus*; and except where
opposed by the horrid and inaccessible mountains encloseth not one, but four entire Provinces, or Kingdoms rather, within its circuit. The
whole length of it, the windings according to
the different scituation of the places considered;
for on this side of *China* in regard of the mountains level ground appears very rarely, is three
hundred *German* Leagues, or twelve hundred
English miles (accounting as *Martinius* doth
fifteen *German* Leagues to a degree) being fortified with Castles and Towers in convenient
places, with Ports near them to issue forth as
necessity requires. The heigth of it is thirty
Cubits, the bredth twelve and sometimes fifteen,
(the *Chinique* cubit being less than our foot by
one only eigth part of an inch) having a Parapet
on each side, for the greater security of those
that pass thereon. In the building thereof three
of ten of the people throughout the whole Empire were continually employed in course for
five years together, and whosoever made any

part

part of it, that a wedg of iron might be thruſt into the joynts of the ſtones, was for his negligence immediately put to death. The foundation of that end of it, which runs into the Sea at *Leotung* was made by ſinking of Ships two furlongs deep into the waves, loaden not with ſtone, but maſſive iron, as it was digged out of the Mine. It is built of great ſquared Aſteler on the outſide, the Core being filled up with flints; was erected in the two hundred and fifteenth year before the birth of CHRIST; and at this very day contemning all injuries of *Time*, remains in a manner without any fiſſure or ſetling. For the defence of it the Emperours of *China* do almoſt alwayes keep ten hundred thouſand men in continual pay. Thus *Martinius* in his *Atlas* of *China*, as I find him truly cited by *Kircherus*.

The other *Hiavouur*, the ſixth Emperour of the Family of *Hana*, is no leſs famous for his Love to learning, and learned men, than for his Magnanimity and valour; and being of a great and excelſe mind, as if the fame of *Alexander* of *Macedon* had arrived at his Court, deſigned to bring the whole World under his ſubjection. But fearing leſt ſome of the Royalets might, during the abſence of himſelf and forces, attempt to raiſe new ſtirs, as ſince his family began to reign they had; he deviſed ſeveral Laws to reſtrain them. Ordaining, that for the future the Lands granted them in right of favour by the former Imperial Decrees, ſhould at their deaths be equally divided, as in *Gavel-kind*, amongſt their children lawfully begotten; whereby in time they became reduced to ſuch penury, as utterly diſabled them, either

M. Mart.
Sin. hiſt.
lib. 8. p. 345

either to maintain the dignity of their Ancestors, or practise against their Sovereigns, as antiently they had done. He ordained also, that upon the Decease of any of them without lawful Issue, their lands should escheat unto the Crown from whence they had originally been alienated.

Having then by these and the like constitutions provided for the safety of his Empire at home, he resolved upon Wars abroad, and by his Lieutenants subdued many Kingdoms of *India*, to the *Chinique* Empire, in that part especially which lyeth towards the South from *Ganges* inclusive to the Kingdom of *Bengala*. But taking afterwards the field in his own person, he brought under his Dominion *Pegu*, the Kingdom of the *Laios*, with *Camboya*, *Cochin-China*, and many other Countries and Islands. And to vindicate himself and Subjects upon the *Tartars*, that were their antient and natural Enemies, and ever ready upon all advantages to infest their borders, as the *Scots* sometimes did ours in hope of spoile; invaded their Countries with three mighty Armies conducted by his Generals; and having put them almost all to the sword, and made about the year before CHRIST one hundred and twenty an absolute Conquest of them even to the North-sea, divided *Cathay* amongst his Captains and souldiers in recompence of their valour.

But these by little and little in long tract of time forgetting the manners and customs of *China*, by perpetual commerce and conversation with the *Tartars* degenerated, and took up their customes; so that in the end, though nevertheless

after

after many Centuries of years, they began to invade their native Countrey. For about the year of our Redemption twelve hundred and six, till when (such ordinary commotions excepted as usually attend great Monarchies) the *Chinois* had lived in continual peace and tranquillity these *Cathaians* conquered *China*. But how? They spent almost, saith *Heylin*, as much time in the conquest thereof, as they did in the possession of it. For after they had reigned therein ninety years only (seventy saith *Martinius*) they were totally expelled again, and were no losers thereby. For, instead of compelling the *Chinois* whilst they had them under obedience to submit to their Laws and Customs, they themselves submitted to the Rites and Manners of those, whom they had for that time subjected ; applying diligently themselves to understand and learn, the Language, Conditions, Arts, and Manufactures of the *Chinois*, which at their expulsion they carried into *Cathay* with them. As the *Romans* did the *Greek* tongue into *Italy*, after the Conquest of *Greece*; and as by their victories in *Asia* (the difference alwaies between civility and riot considered) they brought to *Rome* Effeminacy, Luxury, Prodigality, which were in use chiefly in that Countrey.

This was the most severe misfortune, that ever till that time befel the *Chinois*, after the prescription of so many hundreds of Ages to an indisturbed felicity, considering neverthelefs that the *Cathayans* had a desire by their industrious recovery of them, to maintain the Arts and Sciences of their Progenitors, it could not produce

Heyl.Cosmog. pag.871.

K

duce any great alteration in the manners of the *Chinois*, much less in their MOTHER Tongue.

Here again we may observe; that as the *Israelites* from their first coming into the land of *Canaan*, lived in the height of all prosperity, saving some civil contentions hapning between those of *Judah* and her fellow Tribes, never knew what the fury of a Conquerour meant, till after they had overwhelmed themselves in Idolatry: So the *Chinois* from their first beginning to be a people, having lived in all worldly happiness, the like intestine broiles between their families excepted, never understood what the rage of a forein victor imported, till they also had drowned themselves in the worship of Idols. Both famous Examples, that innovations in Religion are alwaies attended with dreadful judgments.

M. Mart. But let us not omit the accompt, which *Mar-*
Bell. Tart. *tinius* gives concerning this Invasion. In this
pag.1.fol. tract of time the Western *Tartars* forgetting their antient vigour of mind, and warlike spirits, which the pleasures and delights of *China* had mollified, being also weakned by so long a peace, became of a sweeter temper, and received a deep tincture of the Nature and disposition of the Natives of that Countrey. But though I find him thus rendred into *English*, hearken to him neverthelefs in his own words. *Interea Sinicis deliciis fracti, Sinicos induerunt mores, & paulatim fortitudinem Tartaricam dedifcentes, nimiâ debilitati pace, Sinæ evaferunt;* So that you see the *Tartars* became *Chinois*, not the *Chinois*, *Tartars*; whereby

whereby it is most manifest, that neither their Language nor Customs could be prejudiced by this Conquest.

Now you cannot but take notice, that *Martinius* calls those People the Western *Tartars*, which our Writers and divers others call *Cathayans*; and though they have extremely erred thereby; yet nevertheless rather, than on the suddain I should seem to contradict so general an opinion, I have thus far followed them therein; For *Cathay* is no other Countrey, than the six Northern Provinces of *China*, as *Mangin* the nine Southern; which were so named by these *Tartars*, upon this invasion of Theirs; and which *Paulus-Venetus* being personally present in this War accordingly so calleth. And no wonder saith *Martinius*, for by the *Tartars* and *Moors* that use to bring tribute every three years to the *Chinique* Emperour, they are called *Mangin* and *Cathay* at this day.

M. Mart.
Atl. Sin.
pag. 28.

Add hereunto that *Jacobus Golius* in his treatise of *Cathay* tells us, the *Cathayans* and *Chinois* are all one people, and their customs & Language have been one and the same throughout all ages.

J. Gol.
Additam.
de Regno
Cath. pag.
1. *in fol.*

Heylin telleth us, that not long after they had freed themselves from this Enemy, *Tamerlane* with an army of *Tartars* entred *China*, and having won a battle, and taken the King prisoner, upon some acknowledgment of Tribute released him, and quitted the Countrey again, as on the like success *Alexander* the *Great* did the Kingdom of *Porus*. But *Martinius* positively maintaineth, that *Tamerlane* never invaded, nor ever was in *China*, much less conquered, or brought

Id. Bel.
Tart. pag.

it under tribute, *ut perperam quidam scripserunt,*
as some, saith he, have falsly written; for he flour-
ished about the year one thousand four hundred
and six; at which time *Taichangus* Emperour of
China, and the second of the *Taimingian* race
(the *Tartars* being before beaten out of his
Kingdom) governed peaceably all the Provinces
included within the compass of that vast Wall
formerly mentioned.

A. Sem. Until the time the *Chinois* were in such man-
Rel. de la ner subdued by the *Tartars*, divers of the Roy-
Cin.par.1. alets had enjoyed their Principalities; but their
cap.22. victorious Emperour *Humvie* having wholly
expelled the enemy, totally suppressed them
likewise; and about four hundred years since,
united all *China*, as now it is, to the absolute
obedience of one sole Monarch; and not only
re-established in the territories of those *Royalets*
the antient manner of the *Chinique* Policy; but
also adding thereunto many new Laws, brought
thereby the whole Empire into that form of
government, wherein it standeth at this present.

By this union the *Chinois* enjoyed the like *Hal-*
cyon dayes, yea generally, far more the *Royalets*
being extirpated, than their Fore-fathers had
done, for many generations together; until the
J. Nieuh. people after an incursion of the *Tartars* of *Niuche*,
l' Amb.Or. about the year one thousand six hundred thirty
par.2. pag. six falling into rebellion, and not many years
115. afterwards taking *Peking*, where their Emperour *Zunchinius*, having first with his own hands
killed his wife and daughter, in despair hanged
himself in a garden of his Palace; *Usangueius*
his

his surviving General called in the *Nieuchean Tartars* to his assistance; who shortly after setting up for themselves, crowned Emperour of *China, Xunchius* a child of about six years of Age; the son of *Zungteus* King of *Niuche*; which *Zungteus* from his infancy had secretly and unknown been brought up in *China*; where together with their weaknesses, he had learned the manners, sciences, doctrine, Letters and Language of the inhabitants; wherefore he much loved, and was no less beloved again by all the *Chinois*; whose miseries endured in this War, from their own Countrimen the Rebels especially, as in all places it evermore happens where Rebellion once gets the upperhand, are almost inexpressable.

But how calamitous soever their condition was, manifest it is, that they received no prejudice in their MOTHER Tongue or Learning of old. For the *Tartars* upon subjecting and setling the *China* Empire under their own dominion, neither altered the Policy, nor antient form of government; but permitted their *Literati* to govern the Towns and Provinces as before, and left unto them the promotions, and examinations of their Characters, as formerly they were accustomed to enjoy. At which examinations, as the Doctors of the Chaire in the Universities with us, with much more diligence and rigour nevertheless, and indeed with great severity; they appose and make trial what Proficients those that stand Candidates for preferment are become in their Literature and Characters of their Language, in the study of which

K 3 by

by their books written, not only their Learning, but also the Elegancy of their Speech consisteth. So that, if in making their compositions upon such Theams as the Examinator gives them, they write not the Character most exactly true, (being not so phantastical as the *Europæans*, to be weary of their old words, but using all possible means to preserve them in their antient purity) they are dismissed without taking their degrees, how excellent soever otherwise their composures be; with liberty nevertheless to return again for their promotion at the next examinations, which are commonly held at every three years end.

A. Sem. Rel. de la Cin. par.1. c.8.

But of the ratification of these proceedings, and likewise of their antient manner of government by the *Tartars*, *Nieuhoff* in his own words shall more fully satisfie you. *Ils ne changerent ni la politique Chinoise, ni la ancienne forme du gouvernement; mais permirent aux Philosophes de l' Empire de gouverner les Villes, & les Provinces comme auparavant, et laisserent les promotions et examens des lettres à l' accoûtammée.* The same is by *Martinius* confirmed, saying, they changed nothing in their politique government; nay, they permitted the usual customs of the Philosophers of *China*, to govern the Towns and Provinces; they left also the same examens as were used for the approbation of learned men. His own words being. *Stylum Politices Sinicæ modumue gubernationis omnino non mutarunt; imo Sinicis Philosophis, ut antea, regendas Urbes ac Provincias concesserunt; examina Literatorum, ut antea, reliquerunt.* And so far, it seems, the *Chinois*

J. Nieuh. l' Amb.Or. par.2. pag.123.

M. Mart. Bell.Tart. pag.15.

Chinois are from having their antient conftitutions altered by this Conqueft, that he telleth
us likewife, they have already induced the
Tartars to forfake fome of their barbarous
cuftomes, which for many ages together they
had ufed.

Id. pag. 3.

NOW therefore as their *Conquefts* will not,
fo the Commerce and Intercourfe, which they
have had with Nations of a different fpeech, and
which is the main part of *Heylins* objection,
cannot, give change unto their Language, much
lefs branch it into feveral languages, or Dialects of the fame one Language. For by their
Fundamental Laws, the *Chinois* are neither permitted to go into the Countries of ftrangers,
nor admit any ftrangers into their own. *Inter
cæteras leges, ifta caput obtineat, quâ omnis extero-
rum in China aditus intercluditur;* Among their
other laws, the chiefeft, faith *Kircherus,* is that,
by which all accefs of ftrangers is prohibited into
China. And fuch ftrict care is taken for the
execution of this law, that it is almoft impoffible
for any ftranger to remain concealed amongft
them, becaufe his very fpeech, if nothing elfe,
will betray him to be a foreiner; and when
detected, he is immediately apprehended, put
to torments, and if he efcape with life, never
fuffered to return out of the Countrey again.

*A. Kir. Ch
Ill. par. 2.
p. 116.*

Over the door of every houfe, faith the fame
Kircherus, is affixed a Table, or Efcutcheon,
wherein the number of men living therein,
together with their condition is fet down; to
the end that the *Lau-ye* (the *Portugals* ftile them
Mandarines, we may call them Prefects or their

*Id. par. 4.
pag. 148,
169.*

Magistrates) to whose office the knowledg
thereof belongs, may, by a memorable politique
way, understand how many men every City
containeth, aswel for avoiding seditions, as
collecting of Tributes. Therefore, it ought not
to seem a wonder to any, as the same Author
observeth, if that strangers by what means soever at length getting into *China*, are immediatly detected, their hosts being under grievous
punishments obliged to discover them.

And though the Jesuites have of late times
obtained permission to reside therein, whensoe-
ver nevertheless their supreme Moderator in-
tends to send any Novice thither, he is in the
Island of *Macao* first diligently instructed, both to
speak and write the *Chinique* Language, least
being discovered for want thereof, he should
before arriving at their Residency, be impriso-
ned, and the Society thereby put to infinite
trouble and expence to procure his liberty, as
oftentimes even since toleration granted them
they have been. By which toleration they have
so far prevailed upon the Natives, that were it
not for Poligamy, that vast Empire might long
ere this time have been converted to Christi-
anity.

*Id. par. 2.
pag. 117.*

Nor is it only thus criminal, for strangers to
come into *China*; but also, saith *Heylin*, for any
Chinois to go out of the same, all politique means
being endeavoured by them to prevent inno-
vation in their manners, by which the old being
neglected, and laid aside, their antient way of
government might be disturbed, and the safety
of their state endangered. And we read that

*Heyl. Cosm.
pag. 856.*

*A Sem. Re
de la Cin.
par. 1. c. 29.*

this

this in part at leaft the *Hebrews* were command-
ed to obferve, for the fame reafon alfo. For
whenfoever any Nation or People, by intro-
ducing new, alter their antient cuftoms, the
deftruction of that People or Nation not far off
approacheth. Thus the Commonwealth of *Rome*
by taking up prodigality and voluptuoufnefs,
inftead of her antient temperance and fobriety,
loft her liberty. And thus the *Chinois* themfelves,
as you fhall fhortly hear, became fubject to the
Tartars.

Howbeit it feemeth, that the extreme jealoufy
of their cuftomes is not the fole caufe of thefe
reftraints, but leaft by permitting liberty of Intercourfe the wealth and weaknefs of their
Empire fhould be difcovered; for though their
conquefts and civil broiles renders them *effere
ftata gente bellicofa, e di valore*, (to ufe *Semedo's*
words) to have been antiently a valiant and *Id.part.1.
cap.20.*
warlike Nation; now neverthelefs, by their
furfeiting on continual peace, and long enjoy-
ment of all variety of pleafures, no people under
heaven the like, they are become generally effi-
minate; and in regard no preferment is to be
hoped for, but by becoming excellent in their
learning, they all unanimoufly, as it were, apply
themfelves to the ftudy thereof. So that the
foldiery are no otherwife accompted of with
them, than the bafeft fort of people are with us.

But in regard whatever is prohibited, is commonly moft defired.; ftrangers, their Laws notwithftanding, found out a way to creep in
amongft them. For confidering that upon an
Embaffy made by the *Tartars* about the year
forty

forty eight before CHRIST, in tender of their perpetual submission to the *Chinique* Empire, Embassadors might be received; several people under the pretence of the like addresses have oftentimes since gained admittance into the Countrey, and made some trading therein, privately nevertheless, and not otherwise, as *Martinius* informs us. For whereas *China*, saith he, is so shut up against strangers, that no access is easily allowed to any, saving Embassadors; *Turks*, *Laios*, *Samarchandians*, and those of *Tibeth* by land, and the *Siamites* with *Camboyans* by sea, come into *China*; where, under colour of Embassy, they negotiate private commerce. Observe herewith what *Nieuboff* relateth; No man can enter *China* except Embassadors, unless with resolution to end his dayes therein, so strong is the opinion of this people, who for many Ages have been perswaded, that they shall be betrayed and sold to some forein Prince. They cannot traffique with their neighbours without licence from their Emperours; and if they be necessitated to send Embassadors into other Kingdoms, they hardly find any that will undertake the charge; and whosoever accepts the same, is no more or less lamented or bewailed by his Relations, than if he were going to his grave. So hateful is the knowledg of strange countries, and conversation with strangers to them. Either they know not forein Nations, or contemn them, Saith *Martinius*.

But the *Chinois* considering, that these Embassies are but feigned, and that to espy and corrupt them rather, than for any submission

M. Mart.
Sin. Hist.
lib. 2. p.
65.

J. Nieub.
l' Amb. Or.
par. 2. p. 8.

M. Mart.
Sin. Hist.
in Epist.
ad Lect.

of

or amities fake such addreffes are made, give
hem reception accordingly (as from *Martinius*,
Semedo, *Trigautius*, and feveral miffives of their
Society we have collected) after this manner.
So foon as the Embaffador either by land enters
upon their confines, or from fea puts in to any
of their ports, a guard is fet immediatly upon
him, by which (fome few being allowed for his
fplendour and oftentation fake to accompany
him) he is brought unto the next *Mandarine*,
who, the place from whence he came known,
affignes him to the Pallace for him, and his
Retinue to refide in, placing good guards upon
them, leaft any fhould enter or come forth without his licence, all manner of neceffaries, afwel
for provifions as carriages, how long foever they
ftay within the Countrey, being provided for
them at the publique charge. The *Mandarine*
takes a memorial alfo of their goods, which
with incredible expedition by a Currier (for at
every ten furlongs *Chinois*, which make fome-
what lefs than three of our *Englifh* miles, they
continually place one) is fent to the Emperour
at his Court, with the name of the Embaffadour,
from what Countrey and Prince he comes, what
number of followers attends him, and what
Prefents and other things he brings ; fignifying
likewife the great defire that the Embaffadour
hath to make his addrefs unto the Imperial
Court. If by the precife day, according to the
limitation in their laws, no anfwer appeareth
from the Emperour, then the Embaffadour is
prefently fent away again *re infecta*. But if the
Emperour granteth his accefs, then the *Manda-*
rine

rine takes great care, that not any of them be
suffered to pass into the inner parts of the Empire, but directly to the place where the Emperour resideth; and therefore sends him and his
Attendants unto the next *Mandarine*, under
guards nevertheless like Captives, though time
out of mind they have been their Friends and
Allies, not permitting them to see any thing,
much less converse with any man throughout
their whole journey; and at nights, like brute
beasts in stables, they are, under I know not how
many locks and keys, shut up in the Palaces
appointed for them to lodg in. And thus they
are conducted from *Mandarine* to *Mandarine*
after the same manner (as we pass beggars in
England from one Constable to another) until
they arrive where the Emperour resides. Where
commonly after some short attendance, the
Embassadour is led, not before the Emperour,
for he neither seeth, nor speaketh with him; but
the Councel of *Rites* : who by the Royal order
treat with him, and receiving his Presents give
him his dispatch; and of the rest of his Merchandize which he brought, if the Emperour
desireth any thing, he sendeth to see and buy it.
At his departure the Embassadour is rewarded
with much more in value by far than he pre-
sented. This done, and returning to his Palace,
power is given him to vend the remainders of
his goods, which either himself or those with
him, brought with them to the Court; or left
behind at the place where the rest of their company, or Caravan rather, as may be said, were
kept at their first coming to the Countrey. For,

in regard they come but rarely, their numbers
are usually very great; but these are not permitted to enter within the Empire, but for their
abode have some Villages assigned them without the Wall; where having sold their own
wares, they may buy others likewise, so that
they do it in presence of their guards. And when
at length they have made sale of their commodities, and ended their whole Trade, the Embassadour and his company being conveyed to
them, in the like manner as they went from
them at first, they all return very richly laden
to their own Countries again, though by their
Commerce not any thing the wiser for intelligence, nor the *Chinois* one *Jota* the worser either
in their form of Government or Language.

But it may be now demanded, what needeth
all this Policy, this circumspection, or why such
peremptory Laws against the admission of
strangers? When Nature her self seemeth to
have so provided for them, as if she had decreed
they should never have been so much as known,
or discovered to the rest of the World, or seen
by them rather, much less molested with invasions, or corrupted with the access of foreiners.
For, from *Trigautius, Kircherus* telleth us, That *A. Kirch.*
Nature least any entrance should be permitted *Ch. III. par.*
into any to come within *China*, hath, to the *4. p. 164.*
North, and North-west (besides the Wall of
three hundred *German* Leagues) enclosed it
with a vast and endless desart of sand; on the
East and South so munited it with the most
dangerous and yet unknown currents of the
East and South Ocean, with obscure rocks and
unfaithful

unfaithful harbours, as that without manifest
shipwrack, what through the violence and cruelty
of the winds, what through the most impetuous
ebbings and flowings of the sea, the shores are
scarcely approachable. And least from the *West*
any should obtain entrance, behold Nature hath
obstructed the passes and avenues that way into
it, with an unapproachable, inaccessible, and to
this day impenetrable enclosure of mountains
harbouring so many, & such cruelly wild Beasts
and deadly stinging Serpents, as that, with a
certain body as it were of garrison souldiers
she hath so armed it, as from this part no mor-
tal man can ever hope for passage.

But through all these obstructions of Nature
and Policy; both Policy and Nature have con-
tributed the means, whereby not in learned
Greece or pleasant *Italy*, but in the remote and
hitherto unknown *China*, are now at last found
out, the true *Indigenes*, that ever since the flood
of *Noah*, being born and bred within their own
Countrey, never permitted or admitted conversation with forein people. But living contented-
ly at home, in all abundant prosperity, under
their own vines, and under their own fig-trees
their swords being turned into ploughshares
and their spears into pruning hooks, have consumed at least four thousand years without
commixture or commerce with other Nations.

Heyl. Cosm.
pag. 858.
From their demeanor towards strangers *Heylin*
calls them an unsociable people; but whether
they were unsociable thereby or not, certain it is
that their peace and safety consisted therein
Quamdiu ignoti cæteris vixere mortalibus, tam diu
fuer

Fuere fælices; as long as they lived unknown to the reft of mankind, fo long they lived happy, faith *Voffius.* For by once only infringing thefe Laws, and granting liberty of Trade to the *Tartars* of *Niuche,* though but in *Leotung* a Province in the very utmoft North-Eaft corner of their Empire, that war by degrees, and that rebellion took rife, which by afterwards calling in thofe *Tartars,* as was faid, is likely to prove their fatal and final ruin. So dangerous and deftructive it is, to alter the antient and fundamental conftitutions of a Kingdom.

If. Voffius de Ætat. Mun. pag. 46.

Thus hath been fully manifefted, that *Commerce* and *Conqueft,* the two principal Agents in all fublunary mutations, have had no influence to extirpate, alter, or change either the Laws, Cuftoms, or Language of *China.* Neither hath *Time* it felf, which challengeth fo great a Prerogative in the viciffitude of things, had, through the revolution of all Ages, fince the general Deluge, power fufficient to fupplant them. But leaft this may feem to be fufpected, *Martinius* forgets not pofitively to affirm, That the fame cuftoms both at home and abroad; the fame Letters; and the fame fafhion of habit, as of old, they all ufe throughout their univerfal Empire, how far foever it extends even at this day, Hear him in his own words, *Omnes enim domi forifque moribus, omnes iifdem literis, & eodem corporis cultu in univerfo, quâ patet, imperio etiam hodie utuntur. Unde conjectari poteft, quanta fit animorum in iis conjunctio, qui adeo nulla in re funt inter fe diverfi,* whereby may be conjectured, faith he, how great a conjunction of minds there is amongft

them,

M. Mart. Sin Hift. lib. 1. p. 35.

them, that not so much as in any one thing they differ among themselves.

THE objection made by Doctor *Heylin* being now thus fully answered, our subject requires, to give you some accompt of the Language and Letters of the *Chinois*; which (even that little, that hitherto is arrived at our knowledg) in regard of their great Antiquity, & unalterable usage will be found sufficiently enough, to make our Essay probable at least. And about this I shall no longer detain you, than that I may therewith bring my discourse conveniently to a period. Not that language I mean of the Southern and other Colonies, which by nursing up the people in barbarity, through the ambitious negligence of the *Royalets*, is differently pronounced, and from whence it comes to be said, that many Provinces in *China* have a different speech. But their true MOTHER and NATURAL Tongue, which from all Ages hath been used by them in their first plantations, and antient Demeasns of the Crown, and which by their Characters originally composed to the same, is spoken genuinely perfect unto this day. *Trigautius* and *Semedo* call it *Quonhoa*, or the language of the *Mandarines* in regard of the Elegancy, and commodiousness thereof; *Martinius* the language of the *Literati*, not so much because the pronunciation of it is learned by the Natives from their Cradles, as is by some conceived; but for that it is spoken purely and elegantly over all *China* by their learned men, according to their written Characters.

Now considering, it appears from Bishop *Walton*,

Walton, that nothing is more expofed to muta- Bifh.*Wals.* *Intr.ad ling* *Orient.pag.* 12.
tion than Languages, which are in perpetual
floting, as all the commonly known languages
of the Eaſt cleerly demonſtrate; and that the
life of language dependeth upon Letters and
Inſcriptions: for not any thing can more aſſure
us of the alteration and change of the *Hetrurian*
and *Latine* Tongues, and that they differ at this
day, from what they were in times of old, then
their antient Epigraphs, as is thus delivered by
him, *Quantum Heiruſca & Latina hodierna ab* Id.pag.13.
antiqua receſſerunt, ex inſcriptionibus & tabulis
Eugubinis Hetruſcis literis antiquis exaratis, & ex
colitmnis roſtratis, quas nemo adhuc explicavit, cuivis
conſtat. Therefore in regard written records are
ſuch certain evidence, it is my intention in this
ſcrutiny to appeal for the uncorruptedneſs of the
language of *China* to their Characters, which
have remained in writing on record, throughout
all times ſince their beginning to be a people;
and not oblige you to rely wholy upon their
ſpeech, whatever neverthelefs hath or ſhall be
ſaid, to make good, that it continues the ſame at
this day, as primitively it was.

And ſince we are to carry on our Eſſay in an
Hiſtorical manner only, we think it improper
to launch forth into any other kind of prooſes
whatſoever, though (by the way) you are to
underſtand, that whatever arguments of worth
are produced by any Authors for any language
to prove the Primativeneſs thereof, may probably
much more agree to this; of which we ſhall
have occaſion to ſay ſomewhat more hereafter.
And if we ſhould ſay, that the learned Author

L

of the Philosophical Language lately published
hath founded his *Notions* chiefly on the *Principles*
of *This*, we should not happily say amiss; though
for the form of his Character, he hath followed
rather the *Gothique* or *Runique* of old.

THAT the World and Letters are eternal,
Pliny is of opinion. Now, if thereby he meant,
that Letters are as antient as the World, his
meaning, perhaps, might not be far from Truth.
But, that Language or speech, was, before the
World had form; the Scripture warrants. For,
we read; *Dixit, & factum est*, not *factum est &*
dixit: God said before he created, not, created
before he said. Which sheweth, saith *Ainsworth*,
how God created things by his *word*; saying,
and it was; commanding, and it was created;
Psal. 33. *v.* 6,9. and 148. *v.* 5. So that if we are to
understand the Text, *Gen.* 1 .*v.*3. according to the
Letter as he doth; Speech was before either
things, or creatures were made; and consequently is, of more divine Antiquity , than either the
world or men.

That the PRIMITIVE Language was
not a studied or artificial speech, nor taught our
First Parents by Art and by degrees as their
Generations have been , but concreated with
them, is certain. For, we read that God no sooner questioned *Adam*, then *Adam* answered him.
And the Lord God called unto Adam, and said unto
him, Where art thou?   And he said I heard thy
voice in the garden, and I was afraid, because I was
naked, and I hid my self. Gen. 3. v. 9,10. Whereby we are assured, that as the Creation of man
himself was admirably perfect; so his language
was

Ainsw.in
Gen. I.

was originally plain and meek; nothing of that
being found in either, which neceffity afterwards
compelled, the pofterity of the Confpirators at
Babel, for their greater reputation to ftile Art;
becaufe God, having given them over to themfelves, they had no other way left to compofe
and regulate their Actions, then what either
their ingenuity, or experience by enforced and
premeditated means afforded them. And feing
it is prefumed, that *Adam* by his creation knew
whatever might be advantagious for mankind; I
fee, no reafon but we may conceive, that the firft
Characters, that were ever framed to language
were of his invention; for, that they were found
out in the very infancy of the world, is, faith *Sir W. Ral.*
Sir *W. Raleigh* queftionlefs; and the World was *hift. par. 1.*
never more an Infant, than in the daies of *Adam. pag. 67.*
He that gave names to all things, knew beft how
to invent Characters for all things, whereby in
their proper natures, thofe names fhould be
communicated and continued to his Off-fpring.
In like manner, having letters there is no doubt
to be made, but that they had books alfo; for
fome part of the books of *Enoch*, containing the
courfe of the ftars, their names and motions, is
faid to be found after the flood in *Arabia Fælix*,
within the dominion of the Queen of *Saba*
(faith *Origen*, as *loco citato* quoted by our Hifto-
rian) of which *Tertullian* affirmeth, that he had
feen and read fome whole pages. And as little
queftion there is to be made, but that the letters
with which in ftone and brick either *Seth* or *E-
noch*, or both engraved the *Secretiora* of their
inventions, were fignificative and hieroglyphi-

L 2   cal;

cal; such we may say, as were invented by *Adam*
for the benefit of them and their posterity. For,
though in several Authors we find they used
Letters; yet that they or either of them first
found them out appears not in any Author. Seing
then, they are only said to be the first that made
use of them, whereby it is manifest they followed
but a former president, the glory of the invention
remaines absolutely unto *Adam*, unless any man
will go about to yeeld the honour thereof to
Cain; or the first of his issue, before either *Seth*
Dr. Brow. or *Enoch* was born. And though this may per-
Pseud. Epi. haps seem singular, Doctor *Brown* nevertheless
l. 3. p. 223. much inclines thereto; for, having told us, that
many conceive Hieroglyphicks were the *Primi-*
tive way of writing, and of greater Antiquity
than Letters, and that thereby the Language
consisting of things they spake unto each other
by common notions of Nature, he concludes
saying, "This indeed might *Adam* well have
"spoken, who understanding the nature of
"things, had the advantage of natural expres-
"sions.

    That afterwards likewise in succeeding times,
as if they also took example from those engravements, they began to write their learning
in Cyphers, and Characters, and Letters bearing
the form of Beasts, Birds, and other Creatures,
Raleigh, also maintaineth. And it was the best
evasion for all those that suffered from the Confusion of *Babel*, saith Doctor *Brown*.

Purch. Pil-   With Sir *Walter's* opinion herein, that, that
grimage, *Purchas* from *Hiurnius* the *Chaldæan* relates,
lib. 1. p. 82, seemeth fully to consent, saying, that the *Phæ-*
                           nicians

nicians before the *Ifraelites* departed out of
Ægypt ufed Hieroglyphical Characters, which
he thinketh they learned from *Abraham*; the
fame which *Seth* and *Enoch* (mark I pray) had
before *ufed*. As alfo, that *Mofes* received the firft
Alphabetary Letters in the Table of the Deca-
logue, and from the *Hebrews* the *Phænicians*;
who could not want fufficient time to learn and
imitate them, for *Mofes* flourifhed an hundred
years before *Cadmus* wandred into *Greece*. Which
Sir *W.* Raleigh from *Eupolemus* and *Artabanus* Sir W. *Ral*-
confirms, telling us, that *Mofes* found out Letters, *Hift par.* 1.
and taught them to the *Jews*; of whom the *pag.* 268.
Phænicians their neighbours received them, and
the *Greeks* of the *Phænicians* by *Cadmus*. In *Eu*- *Eufeb.præ-*
febius likewife it appears, that *Mofes* firft taught *parat. Eva.*
the ufe of Letters to the *Jews*, and that the *lib.* 18.
Phænicians learned them from the *Jews*; and the
Grecians from the *Phænicians*; *Godwin* attefteth. *T. Godwin*
If then afwel before the flood, as long after it, *Ant. Jud.*
fignificative Characters only were in ufe; for *lib.* 6. c.
without all peradventure that famous Infcription at *Perfepolis* in *Perfia* confifts of fuch Characters; and although it differs, its true from the
received Hieroglyphical way, being compofed
of the form of Triangles feveral wayes tranf-
verted only. Yet we cannot but allow, in regard
the people in thofe early dayes framed the
Characters to their Language correfpondent to
the fancy of their imaginations; but that they
muft be made according to the more or lefs
ingenuity of the People that fo framed them.
And fhould it be ojected that this Infcription
feems fo to exceed all Antiquity, that fome

fuppofe

suppose it may be written before the flood; it
may be answered, that though the world then
had but one *Common language*, nevertheless
according to the divers humours, and capacities
of the People, as hath been said, for they could
not be all alike ingenious, the then *Characters*
might not be general but doubtless different. For,
the *Language* was of God, who is not given to
mutability; the *Characters* were of men, that
are wholy inclined to variety.

And if until the dayes of *Moses*, Alphabetary
Letters were not known, which by violence of
Conquerours, mixture with forein Nations,
liberty of Commerce, long tract of time, desire
of Novelty, and several other waies are aptly
disposed to alteration and corruption. In vain
do we search for the P R I M I T I V E Language
to remain with those Nations whose Languages
consist in Alphabets. For it cannot in reason be
imagined, that Letters could be brought at first
into such a studied order, and methodical way;
but accidentally as it were at random invented
after a plain and simple manner, conformable
to the speech; as all other Arts from small beginnings and ruder notions have grown to
perfection in time and by degrees, many Ages
and long experience being required to perfect
any invention of whatever kind. And if those
Inscriptions reported by *Pomponius Mela*, and
Pliny to have been found at *Joppa*, witnessing that
it was built before the flood; and that *Cepha* or
Cepheus reigned there, and on which were in-
graven the titles of him, and his brother *Phi-
neus*, together with a memorial of the grounds
and

Pom. Mela
lib.1.cap.11.
Plin.lib.5.
cap.13.

and principles of their Religion, had been communicated to posterity in the proper Character,
nothing could have more assured us hereof.
For, our learned *Selden* used to profess, that
for adjustation of time and action, he more
valued one Antique Inscription, than an hundred
arguments of the Schooles. Wherefore it is
much to be lamented, that those worthy Gentle-
men both of our own Nation and others, that
at such hazard and charge have travailed into
the remote parts of *Asia*, from whence all Antiquity is derived; have neglected to exemplifie
some at least of those many Inscriptions, which
remain frequently dispersed in that part of the
World, and which are such, if what hath been
related to me be true, as that they will very
probably confute several Pretenders to this
Title. But not intending to dispute of this;

Certain it is, that there hath hardly been ever
any People so barbarous, or Nation so unciviliz-
ed, which to manifest their Couceptions amongst
themselves, have not had their Characters either
in a significative or Alphabetary manner as the
experience of times and places teach us. By the
Alphabetary kind, as with us, and other nations, aswel in the East, as other parts of the
World, the Vulgar come vulgarly to know
whatever action is performed: But by the significative, those especially I mean, that involved
mystically the whole conception of some certain
matter, the Vulgar came to know nothing, but
what vulgarly befitted them for to know.

Thus, not to mention others. the *Ægyptians*,
Brachmanes, and *Runians* of old, made use of

L 4   Hiero-

Hieroglyphicks to keep their *Arcana Theologiæ & Imperii* fealed up, as it were, in the breafts of their Priefts and Minifters of State only, And thus the *Chin is* invented their firft Characters, and formed them from all things that are obvious to fight; as Beafts, Birds, Wormes, Fifhes, Herbs, Branches of Trees, Ropes, Threads, Points, Circles, and the like; with this difference neverthelefs, that whereas the *Ægyptians,* and the reft invented their Hieroglyphicks to conceale their *Arcana* from the people; the *Chinois* on the coutrary framed their Characters to communicate their *Concepta* to the people. For, as the Characters of *Thefe* were invented for declaring precifely the conceptions of fingle words, and names only, no other myftery being included in them: So, the Hieroglyphicks of *Thofe* did not exprefs fingle words or names, but involved ænigmatically entire *Ideal* conceptions. Whereby the difference between the Hieroglyphicks of the *Ægyptians* and Characters of the *Chinois*, is evident; and that they are not *in omnibus æmuli,* as *Kircherus* would perfwade. But with what other differences are between them, or whether in any manner they may feem to correfpond, we intend not now either to trouble you, or our felves.

THE Inventour of the firft Characters of *China,* was *Fohius* their firft Emperour, who according to the time that is given to the beginning of his reign might be contemporary with *Enos.* For, as hath been faid, *Martinius* and *Voffius* affirm, that the Hiftorical computation of the *Chin s* begins from that year wherein

Fohius

Fohius entred upon his government, which was in the two thousand eight hundred forty seventh year before the birth of CHRIST. Now that year before the birth of CHRIST answers to the five hundred fifty third year before the Deluge, and *Enos* died in the year of the World eleven hundred and forty, which preceded the flood five hundred and sixteen years, whereby *Fohius* might be contemporary with *Enos* thirty seven years, according to the *Chinois* historical accompt, and as by our vulgar Chronology is evident. The most accurate Chronography of the *Chinois*, by the calculation of *Moses*, precedes the deluge seaven or eight Ages; saith *Vossius*. *If. Voss. de Ætat. mun.p.18,*

But I find *Xircherus* very much to dissent herefrom. For, he saith, that the *Chinois* as from their Annals and Chronography may be collected, place the first invention of their Letters almost three hundred years after the Deluge, of which their first King, *Fohius* by name, was the first Institutor; as by the book of the succession of their Kings appears. *A. Kirc. Ch. Ill.par.6. pag.225.*

Now, this variance ariseth, because *Kircherus* for his calculation useth not the same *European*, but a different Chronology from the rest. For whereas *Trigautius, Martinius, Semedo*, with *Nieuhoff*, deduce their computation from the vulgar *Æra* of CHRIST, by which according to the original *Hebrew* Text, the flood hapned in the year of the World one thousand six hundred fifty six; *Kircherus* on the contrary takes his from the *Æra* asserted by *Isaac Vossius*, whereby according to the *Seventy*, the flood is made to happen in the year of the World two thousand

thousand two hundred fifty six; the difference
being six hundred years. And by this computation indeed, we shall find, that the first Letters
of the *Chineis* came to be invented by *Fohius*
two hundred forty four years before the *Confufion of Tongues*; and confequently not much
lefs than three hundred years after the Deluge,
as *Kircherus* hath alleged, the precife time being
two hundred eighty feven years. For *Voffius* to
make good his Chronology affirms, that the
difperfion at *Babel* fucceeded at the birth of
Phaleg, which, faith he, was five hundred thirty
one years after the Flood: *Quam factam effe
diximus ante & poft nativitatem* Phalegi *annis poft
diluvium* 531. being his words.

But although by this it more than manifeftly
appeareth, that *China* had letters, and was
planted two hundred forty four years before
the *Babylonian Confufion*, and that thereby the
Chinois could not be obnoxious to the curfe of
Confounded Languages; neverthelefs (except
their Letters, as *Semedo* conceiveth, were born
with them, and together with their Theology,
taught them by *Noah*) that alfo they were a
people, and confequently had a Language, long
before they could have letters in ufe, reafon
muft grant, and *Voffius* will not deny. For he
informeth us, That his *Serians*, (our *Chinois*
in their Annals record, that in the more antient
times which both preceded, and immediately
fucceeded the univerfal Deluge, their Countrey
was inhabited, though they will not for certain
affirm the fame, but willingly rather acknowledg
their errour therein. But if in them it be an
errour

rrour, then is *Voſſius* himſelf moſt eminently
uilty of the ſame errour. For, he hath long
nce delivered his judgment, that by his calcu-
ation, the *Chinique* deluge correſponds exactly
vith the flood of *Noah.* But unleſs *China* were
eopled, it could not, according to his own po-
tion be drowned. For, with great vehemency
e diſputes, that thoſe Countries that were not
nhabited, periſhed not in the Deluge. Hear
im, *Ut vero diluvii inundationem ultra orbis* ***J.Voſſ.de***
abitati terminos producamus, nulla jubet ratio, ***Ætat.***
mo prorſus abſurdum dicere, ubi nulla hominum ***Mun.pag.***
ædes, illic etiam viguiſſe effectus pœnæ ſolis homi- ***54.***
ibus inflictæ; But that we ſhould draw, ſaith
e, the Inundation of the Deluge without the
mits of the habitable Earth, no reaſon enjoyns,
ea verily, it is abſurd to ſay, that where men
ad no habitations, there alſo the effect of the
uniſhment, inflicted on men only, ſhould take
lace. So that his argument ſtands thus; That
Countrey which was not peopled, was not
lrowned by the flood; But *China* he himſelf
ffirms was drowned by the flood; Therefore
China according to his own affirmation was
eopled before the flood. Either then the *Chi-*
ois are not in an errour for ſo recording, or
Voſſius is in an errour for ſo affirming. But *China*
vithout all peradventure was inhabited before
he flood, and conſequently drowned, and there-
ore both the *Chinois* and *Voſſius* are in the right.
And he himſelf hath furthermore and very
ately acknowledged, That the Chronology of
China, by the *Moſaical* accompt, precedes the
flood ſeven or eight Ages.

Mark

Mark neverthelefs I pray, how learnedly i thus difputing of the Deluge, *Voſſius* occult. pleads the very cafe of thofe plantations, th were fetled before the Confpiracy at *Babel*, an how thofe that were abfent thence could not b guilty of the Crime committed there, nor liabl therefore to the punifhment enfuing there upon.

Now although, which of thefe two compu tations, are, according to the letter of th Scripture moſt warrantable, I will nor prefum to argue; yet neverthelefs what our *Mede* an others have delivered concerning them, I an not to decline. "We know, faith he, the fir "Ages of the Church followed the computatior "of the feventy altogether, though it were moſ "wide of truth; and the chiefeſt Doctors th "Church then had, through ignorance of th "*Hebrew*, for a long time knew not, or believec "not, there was any other computation. H alfo adds, that the great difference which i found between thefe Chronologies proceedeth chiefly, becaufe the *Seventy* tranflating in *Ægypt* voluntarily and of fet purpofe, increafed the years of the firſt generations, to make them reach the Antiquity of fome ſtories of the *Ægyptians*, and thereby exceeded the *Hebrew* computation, above thirteen hundred years. And Doctor *Brown* affirms, "that the *Hebrew* is incontro- "vertibly the primitive and fureſt text to rely "upon, and to preferve the fame entire and un- "corrupt there hath been ufed the higheſt cau- "tion humanity could invent. Wherefore no man fhall perfwade me, no man, I fay, of how great

J. Mede lib. 5. pag. 1094. 1095.

Dr. Brown Pfeu. Epid. lib. 6. pag. 238.

eat Authority foever he be, to believe any
ing that openly contradicts, what *Mofes* hath
livered; which is the moft certain rule of all
ftories, and unto which unlefs we confent, we
nnot confent to truth. However, leaving every
an to liberty of confcience herein; I fhall, with
y principal Authors alfo, proceed with the
lgar *Æra*, as I begunn, in all reverence fub-
itting to the written Word of God according
the *Hebrew* Text; not daring to vindicate
e Antiquities of *China*, fo highly, as with
fius to fay, *Quamvis autem odiofe dictum poffit* $\mathcal{I}$*f. Vof.* *d*
deri, dicam nihilominus, non defuiffe, qui fortius *Ætat. Mun*
s Antiquitates adferuerint, quam alii Mofem *pag.3.*
fenderint.

It fufficeth us, allowing which computation
u pleafe, that *China* was inhabited before the
nfufion of Tongues, that for feveral Ages be-
re that *Confufion* the *Chinois* had the ufe of
tters; to wit, ever fince the time of *Fohius,*
hether likewife you admit him to have reigned
her before or after the flood; and that at this
efent day the felf fame letters abftracted only,
e in ufe amongft them. For we muft obferve,
at the Characters they now ufe were abbre-
ated, from thofe that *Fohius* with other of his
ccefors firft compofed to their fpeech, as by
reherus, having elegantly inlarged upon that,
at others have but hinted at, is manifeftly
ident,

But before proceeding thereunto, feeing we
e thus accidently fallen again upon their Chro-
logy and Annals, I conceive it very pertinent,
let you know the furpaffing care, and nor to
be

be paralleld order, the *Chinois* have from all Antiquity obferved in writing of them, left our following difcourfe chiefly relating to their Language, fhould otherwife feem to receive an interruption thereby.

M. Mart.
Sin. Hift.
lib. 1. p. 20.

Martinius then telleth us, it was of old, and as yet is ufed by this Nation, that the writing of the life and actions of the deceafed Emperour, that it may be free from all deceit and flattery, is by his Succeffour committed to the charge of fom of their moft learned Philofophers, which truly is reputed of all others the greateft honour, and is by their chiefeft men ambitioufly defired. Whereby the *Chinique* Hiftory hath been ever fo continued like it felf, as that, though from time to time as the Ages fucceeded, it be inlarged by feveral Pens, it feems neverthelefs to be the work of one only Author. For, it is unlawful for any but the Hiftoriographer Royal to intermeddle therewith, and criminal alfo, for the Writer of the fucceeding times, to alter the preceding Hiftory.

J. Nieuh.
l' Amb. Or.
par. 2. pag.
104.

In confirmation whereof, obferve likewife the report that *Nieuhoff* makes. The Emperours of *China*, faith he, have evermore laboured to have the Annals of their Empire written by the moft learned of all their Philofophers, whom they chufe and oblige to that end, which makes that people glory, that there is nothing that furpaffeth the truth of their Hiftories, and particularly thofe which are written from the two thoufand two hundred, and feventh year before the birth of CHRIST, unto this prefent time. Wherein their exact care in their Chronology admirably

appears

appears; for, it falls out juftly with the fortieth
fourth year before the Confufion of Tongues, of
which we had caufe though upon a different occafion (when ftating at what time their Empire
became hereditary) formerly to take notice, and
is directly anfwereth to the end of the reign of
Xunus, who firft ordained this order to be perpe-
ually obferved, and who upon the cafting off of
Chus, fucceeded *Jaus*, as is already faid. And it
confirmeth alfo, what *Martinius* afferteth, That ^{M. Mart:}
there is hardly any Nation in the whole World ^{Sin. hift.}
^{lib.1. pag.}
to be found comparable to the *Chinois* for their ^{20.}
certainty in Chronology. *Quâ curâ non ullam*
facile nationem Sinis in Orbe reliquo parem invenias;
being his words. And likewife, left it were not
fufficient for him once only to affert it, he affirms the fame again, faying, *Quâ in re mirabile*
Sinarum femper ftudium emicuit, wherein the ^{Id. pag. 12.}
wonderful care of the *Chinois* hath evermore ex-
celled. Which *Voffius* in like manner attefteth,
frequently calling the fame *accuratiffima Chrono-*
raphia, certiffima Chronologia, the moft certain
Chronology, the moft exact Chronography.

We well know, thofe are not wanting, that
make *Nimrod* to have arrived at *Shinaar* in the
year one hundred and one after the Flood, and
the *Confufion* to have been at *Phaleg's* birth; but
although it is not to be beleeved; as *Voffius* faith, ^{Id. pag. 17.}
that the building of the Tower, the *Confufion of*
Tongues, and difperfion of the people fhould be
made, before fcarcely one Age after the Deluge ^{Sir W. Ral.}
was expired; and though, as Sir *W. Raleigh* tells ^{hift. par. 1.}
^{pag. 99.}
us, "Thefe men do all by miracle, and
beget whole Nations without the help of
"Time;

" Time ; neverthelefs let it be as improbable; and the time as much abridged as it will, even by this computation alfo, the Claffique Hiftory of the *Chinois* begins fourteen years before the *Confufion of Tongues* happened.

It was in the year after the univerfal Inundation one hundred and one, at which time *Phaleg* was born. *Gen.* 11. *v.*16. that the divifion of the Earth, if underftood to be at the birth of *Phaleg,* was made by *Noah* among his grand-children; & that done, that they then went from the Eaftern parts unto the valley of *Sennar;* Arch-bifhop *Ufher* is of opinion. Whereby it manifeftly

Dr. *Ufher* feems, that from their removal out of the Eaft,
*Ann.pag.*3 until the curfe of confounded Languages, what in regard of their tranfmigration, what of the prodigioufnefs of their work, a confiderable fpace of time interlapfed, but what that interval might be, he filently pretermits.

And therefore, if you confult the *Æra,* that fome marginal notes upon our Bible, *Goropius,* Sir *W. Raleigh,* and the moft learned Antiquaries follow, which gives one hundred thirty one

Sir *W. Ral.* years before *Nimrod* came to *Shinaar;* and then
Hiftor.par. if according to *Glycas,* as cited by *Raleigh,* you
*i.pag.*100. add thereunto forty years more to be confumed about bringing the Tower to an height before the *Confufion* enfued thereupon, you will readily find, that the Hiftory which the *Chinois* efteem fo authentique commenceth thirty years before the difperfion at *Babel;* following Arch-bifhop *Ufhers* accompt; and by this other *Æra* obferved by *Raleigh* and the reft it will appear, that the fame hiftory takes beginning eighty four years

before

before the *Confusion of Tongues*, the which in manner accordeth rightly also, with what *Trigautius* & *Nieuhoff* have delivered, that by their Annals it appears they have had the knowledg of one only God, above four thousand years; for we know that from the Flood to this present time three thousand nine hundred sixty two years have elapsed. Now *Nieuhoff* and *Trigautius* follow (I need not repeat it) the vulgar Chronology, and deduce their account from *Jaus*, who began to reign four thousand twenty five years since, and whose memory liveth by these Annals (which *M. Mart.* from *Xunus* seem to be called *Xuking*) *Initium* *Sin. hist.* *ejus libri est Taus Imperator*, that Book takes be-*lib.8. pag.* ginning at the life of *Taus*, saith *Martinius*. From 352. whence we may observe, that though this their History precedes the Flood, it came nevertheless to be written in the succession after it ; which much more contributes to the manifesting of the verity of their Annals, and who this *Jans* might in all probability be. The certainty then of their Annals & Chronology being thus apparent, it remains only to enquire after their Language and Letters, and with what certainty they have been continued.

Alvarez Semedo tells us, That the Language *A. Sem.* which they use in *China*, is of so great Antiquity, *Rel. de la* that many beleeve it to have been one of the 72 at *Cin. pa.1.* the Tower of *Babel*. Of which opinion my self also *cap.6.* will perhaps be, when either any of his Society, or other in his behalf shall make evident, so many Languages to have been spoken upon the *Confusion* there. It is true, that as well many learned men, as *Semedo*, according to the number of

M   names

names laid down in the tenth Chapter of *Genesis*, being seventy, have supposed that the PRIMI-TIVE Tongue was confounded into the like number of Languages. But this, saith *Heylin*, I take to be but a conceit. It being plain, that *Canaan* and his Sons, eleven in all, had but one Language amongst them, which was the *Hebrew*, or Language of the land of *Canaan*. And as for *Joctan* and his Sons, being thirteen in number, considering he was the younger brother of *Phaleg*, in whose time this Confusion happened, it is most probable, and avowed for a certain truth, that either none of them were born, or if they were, yet were all of them too young to have had an hand in the design for the building of *Babel*, and consequently could not be within the curse of *Confounded Languages*. So here is a third part of the seventy to be taken off, as possibly might all the sons of *Mizraim* be, if it were worth the while to insist upon it. With this *Willet*, *Purchas*, *Mede*, and divers others agree. Therefore with them and *Heylin*, I take this but for a fancy, and till made otherwise appear, shall conceive, that the Language of the Empire of *China*, is of far higher Antiquity, and as antient, as the World it self and Mankind.

Some again are of opinion, that the PRI-MITIVE Language was not divided at all into any more or less others, but that the Judgment which fell upon the Conspirators at *Babel* was nothing else, than that their minds, and their notions of things being confused, though they might speak the same words, as they did before, yet they could not understand one another. O-

thers

Heyl.Cosm.
*pag.*8.

A. Will. in
*Gen.*11.
Pur.Pil-
grimage,
*lib.*1.*pag.*
40.
J. Mede,
*lib.*1.*pag.*
38.
M. Caf. ub.
de 4 ling.
*fag.*5.

thers again, that it was a forgetfulneſs of the former ſpeech, and being forgotten, they afterwards
muttered or babbled forth confuſedly, whatever
came next unto their Tongues-end. From
whence it is ſuppoſed the word to Babble, uſed by
us for a ſenceleſs diſcourſe, proceedeth. But whether a diviſion, ſtupefaction, oblivion, or abſo-
lute extirpation, (for what is *confounded* is reduced to nothing) it befel thoſe only that were
There in the Region of *Babylon,* and were either
adviſedly or actually contributors to the building of the Tower. And therefore concerns not
us, who were throughly warm in our goodly
ſeats long before that *Confuſion* happened, and
being not guilty of that crime, could not be
within that curſe, nor ſubject to that Judgment
whatever it was. But to proceed.

In the Language of the *Chinois* the Element,
Syllable, Word, are all one and the ſame; *Idem-
que eſt apud eos Dictio, Syllaba, Elementum* Saith
Trigautius.

N. Trig. de
Chriſt. Exp.
apud Sin.
lib. 1. cap. 5

Their Idiom is very ſuccinct, inſomuch that
as in multitude of Letters they ſurpaſs all other
Nations of the World; ſo likewiſe in paucity
of words they yeeld to all. For the number of
their words ſcarcely exceeds ſixteen hundred.
All of them alſo end in vowels, ſome few excepted which terminate in M, or N, and they
are all Monoſyllables and Indeclinables, as well
Nouns, as Verbs; and ſo accomodated to their
uſe, that many times the Verb ſerveth for a
Noun, and a Noun for a Verb, and an Adverb
likewiſe, if need require; whereby there is not
much pains required to put them together in

A. Kirch.
Ch. Ill. par.
p. 11.

A. Sem.
Rel. de la
Cin. par.
c. 6 11.

Syntax

Syntax: And for the same reason we are assured
by *Semedo* also, that their Language is more
easy to be learned, than the *Latine*, the Grammar only whereof taketh up all our younger
years. Hear him, *Con che si facilita per essere stu-
diata più che la Latina la cui sola Grammatica si
piglia gli anni dell'eta puerile.* Now these being
his words, it seemed very strange to me to find,
that in the Essay towards the *Philosophical Language*, pag. 452, it is said, that upon the accompt
of the great Æquivocableness *Alvarez Semedo*
affirms the *Chinique* Tongue to be more difficult,
than any other Language of the World, quoting
Histor. China Par. 2. *Cap.* 2. But, the truth is, the
Author is too learned to commit such an error
himself, and therefore deserved a more careful
Transcriber; for those words are neither in the
place quoted, nor in any part of *Semedo*'s whole
relation. Who, on the contrary, will likewise
ere we conclude, not from casual hear-say, but
his own long experience, receiving what he
writ, not from the ears of others but his own
eys, attest, that upon the very self same accompt
pretended it surpasseth for sweetness all other
Languages at this day known.

It depends not, moreover, upon Letters disposed into an Alphabetical form like ours, nor
have they in their Language any words compounded of Letters and Syllables; but every
single Character importeth a single word or
name, whereby they had need of as many Characters, as there are things, by which they would
deliver the conceptions of their minds. For
example, if any should go about to render *Cale-*
pine

Kirc.
Wh. Ill. par.
pag. 226

pine into their Idiom, fo many and different
Characters he ought to have, as there are different words therein. Neither do they ufe
Declenfions or Conjunctions, feing all thefe are
involved in the Characters themfelves. So that
it behoveth that man to be endued with a good
memory, that intendeth to attain, but even unto
an indifferent perfection in the *Chinique* Learning. Infomuch that he that by long ftudy,
throughout in manner his whole life time, ar-
riveth to the higheft perfection therein, as alfo
amongft us whilft living we ftill learn, obtaineth
defervedly the prime honours and dignities of
the Empire. And as they are more or lefs learned, fo are they lefs or more efteemed. From *G. Mend.*
whence it proceeds, as *Mendoza* affirms, that *Hiſt. de la*
none how miferably poor foever they be, but *Chin. lib. 3.*
learn at leaft to read and write, it being infamous *pag. 140.*
amongft them to be illiterate.

It may neverthelefs not undefervedly feem
admirable unto any man, faith *Kircherus*, why
fo many, and fuch Characters, which in their
Onomafticon, called *Haipien*, to wit, the Ocean
are numbred at fixty thoufand, fhould be involved as we faid in fo few words, which that
it may be manifeft we are to know, that the
words of the *Chinique* Language, as we lately
fhewed, hardly exceed fixteen hundred. We
may with *Semedo* diftinguifh them. Their Language hath not in all, faith he, more than three
hundred and twenty *vocaboli* [words, I fuppofe
unaccented and unafperated] and of *parole*
[words which though really the fame, differ
in the afpiration and accent only] one thoufand

two hundred twenty eight. But as every of these words hath many and divers significations, so, unless by the different accents they are not to be understood. For, one word signifies sometimes ten, & sometimes twenty several things, intelligible only by the different pronunciation of the Accent. Whereby in regard of the double sence, their Language to strangers is very difficult, and not without great labour, intentive study, and with a thousand reflexions to be learned by them. So that, it is one thing to know the *Chinique* Characters, another, to speak the *Chinique* Tongue. For any stranger that hath a good memory, and diligent care withal, may attain to the height of Learning by reading of the Books of *China*, although he can neither speak the Language, nor understand what the Natives speak to him. From whence may be collected, that as the *Frenchman* writeth, not as he speaketh, so the *Chinois* speaketh not, as he writeth. And we know, that even at this day, in all generally, as well antient, as modern Languages, there is between the reading and speaking a difference either more or less. However, as for that in *China*, *Trigantius* tells us, That all the difference between the speaking and writing consists in the connexion of the words only.

But hereof *Nieuhoff* will particularly inform you, There is no Language, saith he, that hath so many words of a double sence as the *Chinique*, which is apprehensible by the different cadency of the voice. The incommodity received thereby is very great; for one cannot write any thing, that is read to him in this Language, nor of him-

A. Kirch. Ch. III. par. 6 pag. 235, 236.

N. Trig. de Ch. Exp. apud Sin. lib. 1. p. 25.

J. Nieuh. l' Amb. or par. 2. pag. 12.

self

self underſtand a word, unleſs he have recourſe to their Books, to know the double ſence thereof by the Characters, whereby he may readily find it out; when in ſpeaking, he cannot conceive what the Native meaneth. So that, one is not only obliged to have the words repeated; but likewiſe either with Ink to have them ſet down in writing, or if that be wanting, with water on the Table, or ſome other thing expreſſed. This double ſence may in ſome meaſure he apprehended by five different cadencies or principal Tones, which are hard to be diſtinguiſhed nevertheleſs, in regard of their ſweetneſs: One word oftentimes receiveth (amongſt ſtrangers eſpecially) five ſeveral meanings through this variety of Tones. And there is not one word alſo, which hath not one of them, and likewiſe twenty or thirty ſignifications, according to the diverſity of the Aſpirations, which the Natives learn from their cradles, but is very difficult for a ſtranger to attain. And with the reaſon thereof *Trigautius* ſhall ere long acquaint you.

Jacobus Golius conceives the Language of *China* to have proceeded not ſo much from chance and neceſſity, as from meditation and Art. But being it is deſtitute of all thoſe troubleſome aides that are brought in to the aſſiſtance of Art; for they have no Rules either for Grammar, Logick, or Rhetorick, but what are dictated to them by the light of Nature, though greater Eloquence, than amongſt them hath ſcarcely been ever read. Therefore being it is ſo nakedly free from thoſe ſuperfluous guides which we are conſtrained to ſearch after in learning what-

J. Gol. Addit. de reg. Cathaya pag. 7.

A. Sem. Rel. de la Cin. par. 2. cap. 11.

ever

ever other Language; we may well conceive,
that it was at first infused or inspired, as the
PRIMITIVE Language was into our first
Parents, and so from them received, rather than
otherwise invented and taught the *Chinois*. And
whereas some fancy, that it is in many respects
very imperfect, and exceeding equivocal; yet
in regard no Author of credit extant, hath given
us so much as in general terms, any the least
notice of any such imperfections, I may say,
that if any such imperfections shall be found
therein, they relate in regard of the high Antiquity unto Artificialness only. For, without all
peradventure it is a perfectly natural speech, and
was a Language before the World knew, as to
this particular at least, what that, which we now
call Art, meant. And as for the double sence of
the words, those that have long lived in *China*,
those that have diligently studied the same, and
who are most concerned, and can best tell, shall
give you full satisfaction in due place, that this
æquivocableness makes it not only a sweet, but
also a compendious, pleasant, and graceful Language, not naturally defective.

But *Golius* himself shall presently attest it,
verily, saith he, their Language in this is truly
singular, and it is almost incredible, that all their
words are not only Monosyllables, and guilt-
less of Grammatical differences; but also of
such very great affinity between themselves;
that, not otherwise, than by a most fine variety
of pronunciation scarcely perceptible by other
people, they are distinguished. And that
throughout all Ages their speech hath been
one

ne and the felf fame; he formerly affured
s.

Now had he withal faid, that their Charact-
rs were artificial, much Rhetorique needed not
o have perfwaded us into a beleef thereof; in
egard their firft, confifting of Beafts, Birds,
lants, Fifhes, aud the like, could not be made
vithout fome knowledge in *Defign.* Whereby
lfo this Art appears certainly to be, if not more,
t leaft as antient, as Hieroglyphicks. And as for
aofe which they ufe at prefent, though it is
rue, that according as they are written, either
1 a fet or running hand, they yeeld a deviation
1 figure: neverthelefs they are grounded on
ae *Mathematiques* ; for, they be compofed of
erpendicular, rectangular, parallel, and circular
nes, as we fhall fhortly prove, being now obli-
ed thereunto.

The Characters of the *Chinois* are twofold, *An-
ient* and *more Antient* ; or, the Originals and
heir Abftracts. The more Antient are thofe firft
or *primier* Characters of theirs, which we find to
oe of fuch great Antiquity, what Chronology
oever is followed ; and which upon efpecial oc-
ions only, are now in ufe amongft them. And
he Antient are thofe, which from the other were
bftracted, and bearing the very fame fignifica-
ion in their fpeech, are throughout their whole
Empire in general ufe at this day.

Now the firft or *primier*, which, becaufe their ab-
tracts are of above three thoufand feven hundred
years continuance, we have for better diftinction
fake, called their more Antient Characters, con-
fifted of fixteen feveral kinds, taken from the various

rious flyings, goings, creepings, turnings, wind
ings, growings, encreasings, decreasing of vola
tile and reptile things, after the formerly men
tioned significative manner. *Kircherus* thus set
them down.

A.Kirch.
Cb.III. par.
6.p.228,
&c.　The first, from Serpents, and Dragons, and
their various complicatures.

The second, from things belonging to Hus
bandry.

The third, from the Wings of Birds, accord
ing to the position of their Feathers.

The fourth, from Shell-fish and Worms.

The fifth, from the Roots of Herbs.

The sixth, from the Prints of the feet of Birds

The seventh, from Tortoises.

The eighth, from the Bodies of Birds.

The ninth, from Herbs and Water-flaggs.

The tenth, from —— But they seem to b
derived from Ropes or Threads.

The eleventh, from Stars.

The twelfth, from —— But it is a Charac
er wherein of old their Edicts, Charters, an
Letters Patents were written.

The thirteenth, from ——

The fourteenth, from —— But the Charac
ers express Rest, Joy, Knowledg, Ratiocinatio
Light, Darkness.

The fifteenth, from Fishes.

The sixteenth, and last from —— But
seems our Author finding, that his Society kno
not as yet, how to read this kind of them, thin
it needless we should know, from whence Ant
quity composed the same.

Of These (besides what others of their Philo
sophe

hers invented) each of their firſt ſix or ſeven
ᵐperours found out one, *Fohius* the firſt ſort, *M. Mart.*
ᵐ *Imperator Sinicos Characteres reperit, quos loco* *Sin, Hiſt.*
ᵗorum adhibuit, ſed ipſis nodis intricatiores ; The *lib.1.p.22.*
ᵗhe Emperour accidentily deviſed the *Chinique*
ᵗaracters, which he uſed in the place of Knots,
ᵗ more intricate, than the Knots themſelves.
ᵗcherus, as was ſaid, not unaptly, in regard
ᵗheir involvings, tells us, he took them from
ᵗpents and Dragons; as *Jaus*, the ſeventh ſort *A. Kirch.*
ᵐ Tortoiſes, and their ſeveral poſtures : *Sep-* *Ch.IV. par.*
ᵃ *characterum forma ex teſtitudinibus conſtru-* *6.p.230.*
ᵗſignatur literis HIK LM, quos invenit Tan
ᵏ; the ſeventh form of Characters framed
ᵐ Tortoiſes, which King *Yaus* invented, is
ᵗed with the Letters HIKLM. Which are
ᵗ countermarks to demonſtrate how exactly
ᵗy correſpond, with thoſe they now uſe. In
ᵗry one of theſe Characters ſix things were to
ᵗonſidered, the Figure, Sound, Uſe, Significa-
ᵗ, Compoſition and Explication.

Now, it cannot but be here obſerved, *Marti-*
ᵗ ſaith, that their Emperour *Fohius* intro du-
ᵗ his invention of their Characters in the place
ᵏnots; whereby it may be collected, that as
ᵗ *Americans* afterwards, in their Hiſtories, by
ᵗippees, and the *Laplanders* and *Samoeds* at this
ᵗ, in their Exorciſms, by Knots; ſo the *Chi-*
ᵗ more antiently expreſſed the concep-
ᵗns of their minds by the like way. And to *M. Mart:*
ᵗ purpoſe I find, in our Author, that not *Sin. hiſt.*
ᵗch before *Fohius* his dayes one, *Suius* governe- *lib.1.p.19.*
ᵗChina, and that he, inſtead of Characters and
ᵗters, firſt found out knots of Ropes, for eaſing
                                                  of

of the memory, and taught them the right w
of using them in Schools.

Id. pag. 17. Furthermore, it appears by *Martinius*, that th
have a certain sort of Characters in use at th
day, which were invented long before the rei
of *Fohius*. For, *Thienhoangus*, who was th
next governour after *Puoncuus*, and, who fi
civilized, and brought them into order, invent
that double sort of Letters, from which by joy
ing them together, the *Chinois* afterwards, abc
the year before CHRIST according to t
vulgar computation two thousand six hundr
and seventy, framed their Cycle of sixty yea
The first sort consists of ten Letters, which th
call *Can*; the second contains the twelve hou
of the day, which not by numbers, but particu
Characters they express and signifie. From t
connexion of these same characters, they supp
to know, not only the name and quality of t
year, but also of the whole year, and every c
thereof, the secret motions of the Heavens, a
their influences upon terrestrial bodies and i
tural things.

A. Kirc. Ch.
Ill. par. 6.
pag. 226. *Posteriores vero Sinæ rerum experientia doctior*
cum magnam in tanta Animalium Plantarum
congerie confusionem viderent, characteres hujusm
varie figuratos, certis punctorum linearumque du
bus æmulati, in breviorem methodum concinnarû
quâ & in hunc usque diem utuntur; But t
succeeding *Chinois*, saith *Kircherus*, more lea
ed by experience, when they saw the gr
confusion proceeding from such a mass of A
mals and Plants, reformed those character
variously figured, and in imitation of them,

subtract

tracting certain points and lines from them,
iced them into a more compendious method,
ch even unto this very day they use. Now,
the Characters which even unto this very
they use, how many Ages soever their first
racters were invented before, have been
ve three thousand seven hundred years used
them, will very suddenly from warrantable
hority be made good.

f these Characters the number is so great,
hat it is scarcely known. *Martinius* and
edo compute them at sixty thousand; *Tri-*
ius at seventy or eighty thousand; *Kircherus*
eighty thousand, and *Nieuhoff* from *Man-*
us in his History of *Persia*, finds them to be
e than an hundred and twenty thousand. *A.Sem.*
which nevertheless eight or ten thousand *Rel. de la*
sufficient to learn their Idiom, that a man *Ciu. par. 1.*
tollerably converse, and know how to *cap. 6*
te the Characters, and perhaps throughout *N. Trig. de*
r whole Empire, there is not any man, saith *Exp. Chriß*
autius, that knows them all? And when *apud Sin.*
y meet with any that they call a cold Letter, *lib. 1. cap. 5.*
h have recourse to their Vocabulary, as we
urs for any *Latine* word we understand not;
ch evidently declares, that he amongst them,
t knows the most Letters is most learned, as
h us; he is the best *Latinist*, that is best ac-
inted with his Dictionary, or he the greatest
olast that hath read or studied most. The
of their Characters signifies God (their
ngti happily may be intended) as the Cha- *G. Merc.*
ter of the Cross gives beginning to our Al- *Atl. in*
bet, saith *Mercator*, in his Atlas. *Ch. pa. 672*

Now

Now to form all this multitude of Letter
they use nine strokes or touches with the p
only; yet so disposed nevertheless, that by a
ding, diminishing, or turning of a stroke, th
make other new and different ones, and of d
ferent significations. For example, the streig
line marked A, signifies One; being cross
with another line, as at B, it expresseth Te
made with another at the bottom, as at C, it
notes the Earth; and with another at the t
as at D, it standeth for a King; by adding
touch on the left side between the two
strokes, as at E, it is taken for a Pearl; but th
which is marked with F, signifies Creation
Life; and lastly by the character under G,
intended Sir.

A   B   C   D   E   F   G

一 十 土 王 王 王

That their Characters, for Contracts, Polici
Pleadings, and such like transactions betw
party and party, are written with a runni
hand, answering to that which our public
Notaries use; and that for their Manuscri
and printed Books another more set form
observed; as also that some of them are m
difficult, and require more study to be understo
than others, I need not mention; the Chara
ers essentially being still the same. But must
omit the great Antiquity they carry; *Le Lett*
che usano, par che siano così antiche, come le ge
medesima, perchè conforme alle loro memorie Hist

A. Sem.
Rel. de la
Ciu. par. 1.
cap. 6.

e, *le riconoscono da più tre mila sette cento anni, sino a questo del 1640; nel quale scriviamo questa latione ;* The Letters which they use, saith *Seedo,* seem to be as antient, as the People themselves, for perfect notice of them may be taken om their Historical Records, for above three ousand seven hundred years, accounting to e present 1640, in which this our Relation, saith he, was written. Now, as from him is ot to be collected ; how many more, than three ousand seven hundred years, his words *da più* ay imply, so in regard they relate not to their ft or *primier* Characters, but those particularly hich they now use, and to the time chiefly hen they came to be reformed, we have no ed to infist upon them. Though the formerly entioned *plusquam* of *Vossius,* purposely inserted that it may be observed to this end, comprends no less, than five hundred years. Wherere following his assignation precisely, I say, it is lainly manifest thereby, that not only the reucing of their *primier* Characters to a more ompendious method, than formerly they were, apned two hundred thirty four years after the ood ; but also that ever since that their reducement, their Letters have continued without any teration, and are the self same at this instant me, as when primarily they were reduced. In like ianner *Kircherus* throughout the sixth part of his *hina Illustrata* most certainly demonstrates, that very particular Letter of them, bears at this very me the self same signification in their Language s the peculiar *primier* Character, from which it as abstracted, antiently did. And both *Martinius* and

and *Nieuhoff* very late Writers,& by so much the
more unquestionable, have long since declared
that their *primier* Characters were invented al
most three thousand years before the birth of
CHRIST. And indeed, that the Inven
tion of them long preceded their Refor
mation, not any man can possibly doubt
considering especially, setting what hath for
merly been said aside, that being they wer
devised by several persons, succeeding on
another in several Ages, they must of necessit
take up many years of time; before likewif
their posterity could gain so much experience
as to perceive the great disorder attending such
a mass of Animals and Plants, divers years alf
must necessarily elapse, and at last the bringing
of them, being so numerous, into their present
form, in regard of the frequent consultations
mature deliberations, and manifold transcrip
tions, could not in like manner be performe
at an instant. Therefore, without all peradven
ture, their first Letters must be much mor
antient by far than those which they now use
as *Nieuhoff* and *Martinius* have asserted. But i
you incline rather unto *Kircherus*, and the com
putation which he follows, then it appears there
by, that their *Primier* Characters were first foun
out, no less than two hundred forty four year
before the *Confusion of Tongues*, but at what time
or in what Age their Emendation succeeded
is not to be gathered, either from him or *Vossi*

The *Chinois* give willingly great sums of mo
ney for a Copy of their antient Characters we
formed, and they value a good writing of thei
                                    no

now Letters far more than a good painting, whereby from being thus esteemed, they come to be reverenced. Insomuch that they cannot endure to see a written paper lying on the ground, but finding it immediately take it up, & carry the same to the Childrens Schools, where in an appointed place for keeping the like papers, they remain, till afterwards at certain times they burn them, not out of Religion as the Turks, but only out of the love they bear to Letters.

From *Semedo* we have somewhat more to say, *A. Sem. Rel. de la in. par. 1. cap. 6.* *Il Linguaggio] è vario, perchè sono varii li Reg-ni, delli quali hoggi si compone questa Corona, & an-ticamente non eran suoi, mà posseduti da' Barbari, come tutte le Provincie Australi, & alcune Settentrio-nali;* The Language is different, saith he, be-cause the Kingdoms are different, of which at this day this Empire is composed, and antiently did not belong unto this Crown, but were pos-sessed by Barbarous people, as all the Southern Provinces, and some of the Northern. By which it is evidently manifest, that in those Countries which did antiently belong unto this Crown, the speech doth not differ but remains pure and un-corrupted.

And hence it is that *Martinius* throughout his *Atlas* of *China*, when giving us the Chorogra-phical descriptions of their antient Imperial Countries, delivers not so much as one only word of any whatever difference they have in speech. Whereas when describing those other of Northern Provinces together with the South-ern, that not until these later Ages of the World were wholly reduced to obedience of the Em-

N   pire,

pire, and brought into civil order ; he not only acquaints us with their various Language, but also in what manner, and by what means they came to vary therein. For, being as he frequently calls them, rude and uncultivated men, Mountaineers and fierce people, and having been at first *but few*, and no care taken of them, till the main Colonies were peopled, could not afterwards when their numbers were multiplied, be readily brought to submit to the Supreme Soveraignty ; but for many generations through the disloyalty of their Governours stood out, and opposed the same, as hath been already said.

Now, the Provinces which from all Antiquity have belonged to the Imperial Crown of *China*, are generally those that lie on the North of the *Kiang*, where their first Plantations were setled. For *Martinius* informs us, that the old limits of their Empire extended unto that Sea, which we may term the *Evan*. But that as then it was so called, we are not to conceive. On the North *Tartaria Antiqua*, on the South that great River, which they call the Son of the Sea, bounded it. This River commonly called *Kiang*, running from West to East, divides the whole Empire as now it is,

into North and South *China*, being the sometime boundary thereof. He further tells us, that it was of old divided into twelve Provinces by the Emperour *Xunus*. Then into nine by his Successour *Yuus*, before the birth of CHRIST above two thousand, two hundred years ; for at that time it contained the Northern parts only ; from almost the fortieth degree of Latitude to the thirtieth, where the great River *Kiang* gave bound unt

nto the Provinces. Afterwards by little and
ttle the Southern parts were brought under
ibjection, and from barbarity reduced to the
hinique policy. Then at laft was the whole
mpire of *China* divided into fifteen mighty
rovinces.

Whereby it manifeftly appears, that their Lan-
uage continues in its antient purity at this day,
ot in a nook or corner, as the old *Spanifh* in
ifcay; nor in the hilly or mountainous parts of
le Countrey, as the *Arabique* in *Granata*; or as
le antient *Epirotique* in *Epirus*;but throughout all
leir firft Plantations, and Countries which did
ntiently belong unto the Crown, which *Marti-
ius* hath told us,extend from almoft the fortieth
egree of Latitude to the thirtieth, where the
reat River *Kiang* boundeth them.

But, obferve the opinion of *M. Cafaubon* con-
erning the difference of their Language. I con-
:fs, faith he, that in fome fort there may be a di-
erfity in the fpeech of the Provinces of *China*:
ot any man neverthelefs can poffibly think, that
his diverfity could happen, until there were
:veral Provinces, but much more rather, that
he diverfity proceeded from the difference of
he Regions, and the Governments of them.
Vhich is not to be denied; for, we cannot fup-
ıofe, but that their fpeech might come to be dif-
erent, either according to the temperature of
he Air, or as the fcituation of the Province was
nore or lefs mountanous, which naturally cau-
:th greater or leffer rudenefs in the pronuncia-
ion of a Language; or elfe according to the
are in Government, as they were lefs or more

*M.Cafaub.
de 4 ling.
pag.8.*

N 2 trained

trained up in civility, and kept within due order, which accordingly preserveth Language in its purity and perfection. In like manner the conduct of the Plantations, might be of great concernment therein, as when either the new Planters arose from the first swarm, or were of a second or third castling from other places; whilst the head Colony, as may be said, or main body of the Monarchy retained and enjoyed purely their genuine or natural speech. Wherefore admitting; that in those Northern and Southern Regions the Language doth differ, as much perhaps as our Southern, Western, and Northern-*English*, for it will scarcely appear to differ much more, yet it is still one and the same speech. Do we not grant, that the *Greek* was one Language, though there were five several Dialects thereof? And the Language of the *Ephraimites*, *Hebrew*, or *Canaanitish*, though they could not pronounce *Shibboleth?* Otherwise he that lispeth or stammereth, which is a defect in Nature, not corruption of speech, may be said to have lost his MOTHER Tongue. But let the Vulgar Idiom of the *Chinois* be as different as it will, they have not any one Book written therein, no more than we in our Northern or Western Dialects, but all their Books are written in their true ORIGINAL Language, and the Characters of them are, and ever have been one and the same throughout their whole Empire.

Mendoza makes mention of this difference also, and therewith somewhat acquaints us wherein it doth consist He telleth us then, that *it is* admirably strange, that though in the

N.Zhig.in Cyr.Exp. apud Sin. lib. 1. pag. 15.
Cr.Mend. P.st.dell s H.lib.3. pg.239.

Dominions of this Empire, they have several
kinds of speech, nevertheless all generally understand it by the Letters, not Words. But the
reason is, saith he, because one and the same
figure, and one and the same Character, is
common to all in the signification of one and
the same thing, although it be diversly named
in the speech; as for example, the Character
for a City is universally known throughout
their Empire; though in some places they call it
Leombi, and in others *Fù*, the like hapning in
all other nouns. Now, this proceeds not only
in regard their Language is æquivocal through
the divers significations of the Letter according
to the Accent; but also because they have peculiar words for particular things according to
the respective dignity and quality that the
thing spoken of, carries in their speech; as
Semedo, *Nieuhoff*, and *Kircherus* have told us,
and as from *Martinius* you will very suddenly
hear. And therefore *Mendoza* ought to have
declared what kind of City the *Chinois* intend
by *Leombi*; for, what manner they mean by *Fù*
will appear ere long. And of all of them the
words are perfect *Chinois*, and after the purity
of their Idiom pronounced accordingly. As in
like manner with us, though in the North of
England they call that a *Dove-cote*, which in the
South is called a *Pigeon-house*, the names nevertheless are good *English*; So also *Ensis* is as true
Latine for a Sword as *Gladius*; and ᾽αϛεϊόλης as
pure *Greek* for *Urbanitas* as ἐυἰϱϵφπϵλϊα. But to
our purpose *Cheu* is as uncorrupted *Chinique* for
a City as *Fù*, and *Hien* as either; the diversity

M. Mart.
Atl. Sin.
p. 108.

of Terms proceeding from the different dignities they bear. For, thus faith *Martinius*, The
Chinois call not the greater Cities *Fù*, but *Cheu*,
and those lesser ones which are under their
jurisdiction *Hien*. They call a Royal City also
Kingsu, for as the same Author hath it, it is to
be observed, that *Kingsu* is the common name
of dignity for their Regal Cities, but not for
any one properly and singularly so called. But
to what degree of Cities *Leombi* answers, I
cannot find, unless happily it might be mistaken for *Ningpo*, a Port Town, which the *Por-*
Id. p. 118.
tugals as *Martinius* informs me, are wont by
somewhat a corrupt name to call *Liampo*.

Whereby it is observeable that by one only
word they express that, which we are enforced
to signifie by divers. As thus also, for to say
A Sem.
Rel. de la
Cin. par.
cap. 6.
amongst us *Europæans* the manner of taking
any thing, either with the whole hand, or with
some particular fingers thereof, we are alwaies
obliged to repeat the Verb *Take*, amongst the
Chinois it is not so, for each word signifies the
verb, and the manner likewise. For example,
Nien, to take with two fingers: *Tzo*, to take
with all the fingers: *Chuà*, with the whole
hand turn downwards: *Toie*, with the hand
open turned upwards. So also with the verb,
Is, whereas we say, He is in the house; He
is eating; or He is sleeping: They have a
word, wherewith at once they express, both
that He is and the manner how He is. We to
say the foot of a *Man*, the foot of a *Bird*, or the
foot of any *Beast*, are alwaies necessitated to
specifie it with the same word foot; but the

Chinois

Chinois do it with one single word ; as *Kio,* the foot of a Man : *Chuá,* the foot of a Bird : *Tbi,* the foot of any Beast whatsoever.

The Natives of *China* speak generally as from their Infancy they are taught, without observing any Accents at all ; whereby in divers places the People, like our countrey Peasants, as they afterwards attain to a more or less habit of civility and learning speak finer, or broader, and with a fuller mouth than others. For, it may be collected from *Martinius,* that he among the *Chinois* that is not well read in the Language, and understands not the Characters rightly, *ore loquentem rustico,* speaking in a rustical manner, delivers his mind harshly ; whereas he that is learned in them pronounceth his words with a grace genuinely. To *These* the Language is familiar ; from *Those* not so welcome or commendable. *M. Mart. Sin. Hist. lib. 7. pag. 276.*

Thus in the Province of *Chekiang,* that which the *Literati* after the elegant manner of the speech incorruptedly call *Kingsu,* the vulgar sort of people speaking after the common way less exactly, call *Kingsai* ; from whence in *P. Venetus* the name *Quinsai* springeth. So likewise in *Fokien* where they speak clownishly they usually change N, into L, as *Lankin* for *Nankin,* and the like. For thus *Martinius* also, in his description of *Nankin.* The *Portugals,* saith he, vulgarly call it *Lankin* receiving the errour from the *Fokiens,* with whom they chiefly trade ; for these being very rude in speaking by a most common vice of their Countrey are wont to change every N into L. After the same man- *Id. Atl. Sin. pag. 110.* *Id. pag. 95*

ner

-ner, as in the East of *England* they say a *Chim-Ney*, and in the West a *ChimLey*; or as with us in several parts of *Somersetshire*, S, is changed into Z; as *Zuch* for Such; and F, into V, as *Vather* for Father and the like. Where also many of the People, the farther West especially, speak so confusedly in the mouth, that he, that is not acquainted with their Idiom, can hardly understand either what they mean or say; though nevertheless, that which they speak is *English*.

Those people of *Fokien* are the only they almost of all the *Chinois*, that adventure to go to sea and trade; and that *non obstante* the Laws of the Empire maintain free *Commerce* and *Intercourse* with forein Nations; whereby they

M. Mart. use not all, saith *Martinius*, one and the same
Atl. Sin. speech, but in several Cities it differs, insomuch
p. 121. that hardly and with difficulty one understands another, the polite elocution of the *Literati* common to all the other Provinces, being less known and used here, than in any place else.
Id. p. 128. But in *Jenping* and the territories belonging to it (for every Province hath several, as great as some of our *European* Kingdoms) which was planted by a Colony from *Nanking*, the Inhabitants speak as the *Literati*, which in regard they live amongst such rusticks is accompted
A. Sem. Ril singular in them. Now, *Semedo* in celebrating
de la Cin. p. the *Chinique* speech will assure you, that at
1. cap. 6. *Nanking* it is spoken purely. His words being, *Hanno più del soave che dell' aspro, e se si parla perfettamente, come d'ordinario si ode in* Nankin; *lusinga l udito;* Their Language, saith he, is more sweet than harsh, and if it be spoken perfectly,

ctly, as it is ordinarily at *Nankin*, it flattereth
the attention of the Auditors, or is very delightful to the Ear. As our *English* Translation hath

By all which it appears, that from the diffe-
ent appellations given to one and the same Cha-
acter, and the divers pronunciation of their
Characters in divers places, though the words
re the very same, the diversity of their Language
proceedeth. Therefore to make an end of this dif-
erence at once for all; The natural roughness of
he Regions, attended by the ambitious proceed-
ngs of the *Royalets*, in those Provinces where
hey domineered, causing a rough nature in the
nhabitants made them live like Barbarians, and
peak accordingly; whilst the pure Language
f their Ancestors lay neglected, and their mo-
ality trampled in the dirt. But what through
heir beginning to be reduced to the Imperial
Diadem by *Chingus* first, and afterwards by *Hia-
ouus* about an hundred and forty years before
he birth of CHRIST; what through their
inal reducement and union to the Crown, by
he victorious *Humvu*, as was said; their antient
Language hath taken root again, & spreads it self
hroughout all those united Provinces, though
ach of them nevertheless still retains their so
udely ingrafted speech, as being by long time be-
ome habitual and natural to them; and not in
possibility on the sudden to be easily either refined
or reformed. So that with *Semedo* we may confi-
ently say; it is so far from being lost, that though
he Language in those Provinces by their re-
volts became different, it returns again by their
Union

Union into one only throughout the whole *Chinique* Empire. *Però la lingua della Cina venne essere una sola, che chiamino Quonhoa, ô lingua di Mandarini; perche essi con l'istesso passo col quale inducevano il lor governo in altri Regni, introducevano anche la lingua: e così hoggi corre per tutto il paese, come il Latino per tutta l'Europa; anzi più universalmente, conservando anche ciascuno la sua natural favella.* Therefore, saith he, the Language of *China* comes to be one only, which they call *Quonhoa*, or Language of the *Mandarins*; for with the same pace as they introduced their Government into those other Kingdoms, they brought in their Language also; and so it runs throughout the whole Countrey at this day, as the Latine throughout all *Europe*. but more universally, every one likewise keeping their natural, or clownish manner of speech as *Nieuhoff* calls it, by which the Inhabitants of one place scarcely understand one another, as was instanced in the Province of *Fokien*, unless they have recourse to their Books and Characters, which are all one and the same, whereby they readily comprehend the sence and meaning of him that speaketh. Hence it is, that we *Europeans* endeavour wholly to perfect our selves in the Language of the *Literati*, because it is more easie and more general; for thereby saith *Trigautius*, Strangers may converse with the Natives in any Province. Hence it is, that the style they write, is far different from that they speak; although, saith *Semedo*, (and mark him, I pray) the words are the same, so that when one goeth about to write, he had need to recollect his wits,

for

Marginal notes:

y. Sem. Rel. de la Cin. par. 1. cap. 6.

J. Nieuh. T Amb. Or. par. 2. pag. 13.

N. Trig. de Ch. Exp. apud Sin. lib. 1. p. 28.

A. Sem. Rel. de la Cin. par. 1. cap. 6.

or he that will write according as commonly
they speak, may worthily be laughed at. Hence it *G. Mend.*
, that *Mendoza* telleth us, the Language of the *hist. della Chi.lib.1. p. 159.*
hinois, is, as the *Hebrew*, better underſtood by
writing then ſpeaking, the Characters being diſtinguiſhed by points, which ſerve not ſo com-
modiouſly for ſpeech. And hence it is, that *Tri-* *N.Trig.de Ch.Exp.*
autius, giving us another reaſon for it, ſaith, I do *apud Sin-*
erily beleeve, that the cauſe thereof is, for that *lib.1. p.37.*
from all memory of Ages, this people have endea-
ored to write elegantly rather than ſo to ſpeak,
inſomuch that all their Eloquence even to theſe
our dayes conſiſts, not in pronunciation but
writing only. *Hic porro ſcribendi modus, quo ſin-*
gulis rebus ſingulos appingimus characteres, etſi me-
moriæ ſit permoleſtus, tamen adfert ſecum inſig-
nem quandam noſtriſque inauditam commoditatem,
&c. But although this way of writing, whereby
we are, ſaith he, to ſet down a particular character for every thing, be extremely troubleſome
to the memory, yet it brings with it a certain famous and incredible advantage to us, in regard
of the univerſality of the Letter. Which incredible advantage, that as well the whole World, as
we *Europæans* may enjoy, our learned Dr. *John*
Wilkins by the propoſal of a *Real Character* hath
made a fair overture lately, and if others would
as willingly contribute their ſtudies, as he hath
ingeniouſly begun; for no humane invention,
but Divine creation can make any thing perfect
in the ſudden; we might no longer complain
of the unhappy conſequences that ſucceeded the
Confuſion at Babel, nor *China* glory that ſhe a-
lone ſhall evermore triumph in the full fruition
of

of those abundant felicities that attended mankind, whilst one common Language was spoken throughout the World.

Now, though it is not to be denied but that Language precedes Letters, for we speak before we can either read or write, nevertheless it must be granted withal, that we could neither write nor read, unless Characters had been framed to Language. And Characters were at first framed to Language, not only that by them, the actions of the respective people might be commemorated, but also that by such commemoration the Language it self should be preserved to Posterity. Therefore the certainty of Language consists not so much in the speaking and pronouncing, as in the reading and writing : not in the words but Letters. For thus, he that is wel read in the Oriental tongues, we declare to be a great Linguist, as being learned in the speech of the Eastern Nations. By which it manifestly appears, as Bishop *Walton* formerly asserted, that by Inscriptions the truth of Language is discovered. Now *Nieuhoff*, *Vossius*, and others have assured us, that the *Chinois* can and will in maintenance of the truth of *Theirs* produce faithful witnesses, Antient Records written from Age to Age in not Alphabetary, but significative Characters, such, as the World in the Infancy and Nonage thereof had in use, & such as *Martinius*, *Semedo*, & our *Chinique* authors have generally affirmed, are the same at this very day, as when primitively they were invented : which eminently convinceth that their Language remains as pure and uncorrupt at this present in those Characters, as when they first began to have a Language.   But

But the Reverend Bishop proceeds farther, and positively, as formerly cited, concludes, saying, *Idcircò linguæ omnes, quas libri scripti à communi clade non servant, vicissitudini, ut omnia humana, semper obnoxiæ sunt, & singulis sæculis insignem mutationem subeunt*; Wherefore all Languages that written books have not preserved from common ruin, are, as all humane things, ever obnoxious to change, and in every Age undergo a notable mutation. Whereby it is more manifestly evident (And to this end especially he thus delivered his judgment) that such Languages which have been preserved in written books are not subject to change. And therefore, finding from those Authors that living many years in *China*, have not only been eye witnesses, but also day and night most studious in their Antiquities (*Martinius* professing that for ten years together, except for his set prayers, he never took any book in hand but *Theirs*) finding I say from such unquestionable Authorities; That the *Chinois* have been a people ever since the flood of *Noah*, and before the *Confusion* of Tongues ; That their Language hath continually in all times , from their first beginning to be a Nation, been preserved in written books; *That* the Characters wherewith those books be written, are the self same, which from all Antiquity were extracted from their Original Hieroglyphicks: *That* in those Characters their Language hath ever since consisted, and according to them, is at this present day spoken purely: And *That* by the same Characters their Language is generally,

N. Trig. de Christ. Exp. apud Sin. lib. 1. pag. 3 M. Mart. Sin. Hist. in Epist. ad Lector.

and

and univerfally underftood throughout the whole *Chinique* World, We may fafely conclude that the MOTHER or NATURAL Language of the Empire of *China*, perdures in its Antient purity without any change or alteration.

And I muft not omit, that feveral books yet live amongft them, written in their firft and original Hieroglyphicks, which ftill remaining in their Libraries, are underftood by all their *Literati*, though they are no longer uſed, except in fome Infcriptions, and Seals inftead of Coats of Arms. Among thefe fort of Books is extant one called *Yeking* of great Antiquity, as taking beginning with *Fohius*, and of as great efteem for the *Arcana* it contains. This Book feems much to confirm the opinion of thofe, that would have the Infcription at *Perſepolis* more antient than the flood. For, as *This* in *Perſia* confifts only in Triangles feveral wayes tranf-verfed: So *That* in *China* confifts only of ftreight lines feveral wayes interrupted. It treats efpecially of Judicial Aftrology, Politique Government, and occult Philofophy.

A.Kirch.
Ch.Ill. par.
6.p.228,
A.Sem.Rel
de la Cin.
par.1.c,6.
M. Mart:
Sin. hiſt.
lib.1.p.16.

But fome may perhaps fay, that with the change of their Antient Theology, the *Chinois* might change their Language alfo. But this Argument is of no validity at all; for, it may as well be faid, that the *Ifraelites* becaufe they fet up the *Golden Calfe* in the Wildernefs, loft their natural Tongue; or at leaft when under *Jeroboam*, ten whole Tribes making a defection followed the like Idolatry. But to come nearer home, every man knows, that our felves changed

our

ur Religion in the time of *Edward* the sixth;
et not any man knows, that thereby our speech
eceived an alteration. Besides the *Chinois* did
ot so totally fall from their Antient Theology,
ut that (as hath been said) they have *Xangti*,
heir being infected with Idolatry notwith- N. *Trig. de*
tanding, in as great veneration at this day, as *Christ. Exp.*
b antiquo; also their *Literati* not only not *apud Sin.*
vorship, but likewise have no Idols, still ado- *lib.1.p.105*
ing one only Deity, by whom they beleeve all
hings here below are governed and preserved;
nd they use the same Language now, as when
hey first were taught to adore one God only,
which according both to *Trigautius* and *Nieuhoff*
s above four thousand years since.

NOW, in regard that those who have written of the PRIMITIVE Tongue, may be
observed to recommend unto us six principal
guides to be directed by, for the discovery
thereof; viz. *Antiquity, Simplicity, Generality,
Modesty of expression, Utility,* and *Brevity,* to which
by some is added *Consent of Authors* also; We
having already spoken sufficiently, as to the
Antiquity, will consider in what degree the
Language of the *Chinois* may correspond with
the rest of these Remarques, and then submit
our selves to censure.

First then as to *Simplicity*, our *Chinique* is a
Language that consists (and it is singular therein) all of Monosyllables, not one Dissyllable,
or Polysyllable being to be found in it; nor hath
it any Vowels or Consonants, but a peculiar
Hieroglyphical Character for what ever can be
conceived, either in the mind, or may be obvious

to

to the sence. And if in this our Essay you have
met with some words of many syllables, note
nevertheless that every syllable is a particular
word, but because that divers syllables are taken
to signifie one only thing, those which we have
had occasion to mention herein, are by us con-
nexed after the manner of our speech in *Europe*.
And although the *Chinois* have as many Characters as there are things, they know nevertheless
so well how to joyn them together, that they exceed not above seventy or eighty thousand, as
you have heard.

N. Trig. in
Exp. Chrift
apud Sin,
lib.1.p.26.

Neither doth their Language consist, saith
Martinius, as ours, of any certain Method, or
order of Alphabet, but every thing hath a figure,
by which it may be differently expressed from
others, composed by no Art or Rule, and as it
were by chance attributed to the subject-mat-
ter; and fitted, as I may add, to the Infancy and
Simplicity of Time. Furthermore the *Chi-*
nois are never put to that irkesome vexation of
searching out a *Radix* for the derivation of any
of their words, as generally all other Nations
are; but the *Radix* is the word, and the word
the *Radix*, and the syllable the same also, as *Tri-*
gautius hath long since affirmed; which per-
swades a facility in their speech not to be paralleld by any other Language, and that the true,
genuine, and original sence of things seems to
remain with them. Besides they are not troubled with variety of Declensions, Conjugations,
Numbers, Genders, Moods, Tenses, and the like
Grammatical niceties, but are absolutely free
from all such perplexing accidents, having no
other

M. Mart.
Sin. hift.
in Epift. ad
Lector.

other Rules in use; than what the light of Na-
ure hath dictated unto them; whereby their
Language is plain; easie, and simple, as a NA-
TURAL speech ought to be. And it is worthy
observation, that, whereas, in point of Theology, they of all other people have been least guided by the light of Nature; in point of Language;
they of all other people have been most, yea, on-
y guided by the light of Nature. But it was Na-
ure that from God taught them their Language,
and it was the God of Nature, that by *Noah*
taught them their Theology.

Moreover, the Letters, then which nothing can
be more certain, testifie, that it is *sine u'la vocum
peregrinarum mixtura,* without any mixture of forein words. The *Hebruitians* would have us accept
the same account of the *Hebrew* ; and therefore
well knowing how superstitiously our Divines for
the most part are affected towards the *Hebrew*
Tongue, and that they will not allow it to be the
Language of *Canaan,* but the *Original* Speech; we
leave them to enquire, whether the Language
of the *Chinois* (whose twelfth sort of their first
or *Primier* Characters, seem in no mean degree
to correspond even with the now *Hebrew* Letters) may not be the really true, pure, and antient *Hebrew* Tongue. Which they say was lost in
the time of the Captivity, or as others rather before the entrance of the *Israelites* from *Ægypt*
into the land of *Canaan.* For, (let their Language be what you please) if it became utterly
forgotten, in the seventy years their Captivity
endured, much more questionless might it be corrupted in the some Centuries of years during

O   their

their affliction in *Ægypt.* When the Taskmasters
that *Pharaoh* and his Councel set over them were
Ægyptians, the Text being plain, that, *They did
set over them Taskmasters to afflict them with their
burthens,* Exod. 1. v. 11. *and* Exod. 5. v. 14. When
to encrease their afflictions the more, they lived
dispersedly over all the land of *Ægypt, So,* saith
*Moses, the people were scattered abroad throughout all
the land of Ægypt, to gather stubble instead of straw.*
Exod. 5. v. 12. When that Text also, *Speak now
in the ears of the People, and let every man borrow
of his neighbour, and every woman of her neighbour
Jewels of silver, and Jewels of Gold,* Exod. 11. v.
2. sheweth, that not only they lived promiscuous-
ly among the *Ægyptians* ; but likewise used the
Ægyptian Tongue, how else could their neighbours (*Ægyptians* saith *Aynsworth*) understand
what they desired to have, unless either they
spake the language of the *Ægyptians,* or the
Ægyptians theirs, whatsoever it was ? And
when they went up from thence accompanied
with a mixt multitude ; *And a mixed multitude
went up also with them.* Exod 12. v. 38. Which
were *Ægyptians* and other Nations, saith *Aynsworth,* but the *Chaldee* Paraphrast many strangers, whose numbers *Willet* finds to be not fewer
than five hundred thousand persons, that having
either lived in *Goshen* with the *Israelites,* or drawing together with them from the several parts of
Ægypt accompanied them from thence, being
moved by the works of God to go out of *Ægypt*
with them. And in regard these had so great an
influence upon them, as in so short a time after, to
corrupt their ways by making them to murmure
                                                    again

*Ainsw. in
Exo. 11. and
12.
Willet in
Exod. 12.*

gainſt God, and luſt after fleſh, *Numb.* 11. It
nay not be improbable, but by their long and
onſtant continuance amongſt them, they
night contribute much to the corruption of
heir Language in like manner ; they being rea-
ily prone, as by their frequent Rebellions it ap-
ears, to entertain any thing, how pernitious
ever to their ſucceeding generations.

Cluverius as I find in M. *Caſaubon*, uſeth it as
n argument in oppoſition to the Antiquity of
he *Hebrew* Tongue, that almoſt a thouſand
ords may be collected therein, which to moſt
r many Languages at leaſt are common. But
ow many ſoever *Cluverius* hath collected thoſe
oreign words to be, I ſhall now remember one
nly, *Ophir*, from whence *Solomon* had his Gold,
retious Stones, Ivory, and other Rarities; in re-
ard eſpecially Writers ſo much differ concerning
. Some taking the ſame for pure Gold it ſelf; O-
hers ſuppoſing it to be that Region of *America*,
vhich is commonly called *Peru*, and of which
here being two, the North and the South ;
hey will have them to be joyntly called *Par-*
aim, and that gold, the gold of *Parvaim* : Others,
eph ala or *Sophila* in *Æthiopia*; Others again an
Iland in the *Red Sea*; and Others *Hiſpaniola*. Now
hat which hath cauſed this diverſity of opinions,
nd that the place hath hitherto been unknown,
s, the miſtaking of *Ophir* to be *Hebrew*, when
ndeed it is an *Ægyptique* or *Coptique* word, and
mongſt the *Ægyptians* of old was the name for
India, and no other place whatſoever.

But if this mixture of words may be brought
a bar againſt the *Hebrew*, what judgment ſhall

M. Caſaub.
de 4 ling.
pag. 33.

A. Kirc. Ch.
Ill. par. 2.
pag. 58, 59

be given in behalf of that people, which have e-
ver since the universal flood used a speech, that hath
not any one word thereof common to other Languages ; such Countries as have been subdued,
or such Colonies perhaps as have been planted by
them excepted ? And if ever our *Europæans* shall
become throughly studied in the *Chinique* tongue,
it will be found, that not only the *Chinois* want
words to other Languages common, but also
that they have very many whereby they express
themselves in such Elegancies, as neither by *Hebrew*, or *Greek*, or any other Language how elegant soever can be expressed. Besides, whereas
the *Hebrew* is harsh and rugged, the *Chinique* appears the most sweet and smooth Language, of al
others throughout the whole World at this day
known.

And as if all things conspired to prove thi
the PRIMITIVE Tongue. We may ob-
serve, how forceably Nature struggles to demon-
strate so much. The very first expression we make
of life, at the very instant minute of our Births, is
as was touched on before, by uttering the *Chiniqu*
word *Ya*. Which is not only the first, but indeed
the sole and only expression, that Mankind from
Nature can justly lay claim unto.

The Language of *China* as hath been shewec
also, consisteth all of Monosyllables, & in our In
fancy, the first Notions of speech we have are al
Monosyllables ; as *Ta*, for Father; *Ma*, for Mother
Po, for Brother; the like happening in all othe
terms, until by hearing and observing what o
thers in our *confused Language* say, we alter ac
cordingly, adding now and than a Letter or Syl
l. b'

able by degrees ; whereby in the end we are
brought to plain words. For, it is not by natural
inſtinct, but by imitation, and as we are inſtruct-
ed that we arrive at ſpeech , that is, in ſimple
terms and words to expreſs the open notions of
things, which the ſecond act of Reaſon com-
poundeth into propoſitions, and the laſt into forms
of Ratiocination.

The *Chinois* have not the Letter R, nor can
ever by any poſſible means be brought to expreſs
or pronounce the ſame, whatever labour or diligence is uſed by them. And when our Children
attain to riper Age ; as if Nature abhorred the
Confuſion, what care and pains do we take, what
opportunities not lay hold of, by practiſing and
repeating to make them pronounce this Letter,
till education after long conteſt prevailing they
arrive thereat ? Thus from our *Births* to our *Infancy*, and from our *Infancy* to *Riper Age*, till Nature is compelled to yeeld by the enforced power of inſtruction, unto corrupt ſpeech, we generally throughout the Univerſe appear in our
Language direct *Chinois*.

But peradventure here likewiſe ſome will be
ready to ſuggeſt, that the Language of *China* is
not plain and eaſy, but difficult, not to ſtrangers
only, but the Natives alſo, in regard of the
divers Accents and great Æquivocation of the
words proceeding from them. To which is anſwe-
red, that let the difficulty be ſuppoſed as great
as thought may think, or Art can make, it relates
unto ſtrangers ſolely ; and therefore cannot in
the leaſt degree reflect upon the Primitiveneſs
of the ſpeech ; becauſe when the whole World

J. Nieuh.
l' Amb. Ort.
par. 2. pag.
13.

O 3   had

had one common Language; throughout the
whole World none were strangers to that Language; but all people universally understood and
spake the same, being born Natives thereof,
and learning it from their *Mothers* breasts, as
the natural *Chinois* now do, or as any other
Nation ever did theirs. It was the *Confusion of
Tongues*, that first made strange Languages, and
Strangers to them, whereby they became difficult to be attained. But afterwards, when
either curiosity invited, or necessity compelled
men to learn them, Art entred to act her part
therein, and by methodical wayes, and orderly
Rules sweetned difficulty, and induced her to
submit to diligence, which after much study
nevertheless prevailed; and finally got the
upper hand.

And this *China* it self shall witness, for *Pr.
Jacobus Pantoya* finding it absolutely necessary
for propagating of the Gospel, to know the true
Idiom of the Language, framed our *Europæan*
musical notes UT, RE, MI, FA, SOL, LA,
to answer in pronuntiation unto the elevations
and cadencies observable in the *Chinique* Accents
which are these,

A   V   U   O

A. Kirch.
Ch. III. par.
1. p. 12.
The first Accent A answers to the Musical
Note *U T*: but the *Chinique* sound or pronunciation, denotes the same, and it is the first pro-
ducing an equal voice.

The second, ——— answers to *R E*, and a-
mongst the *Chinois*, it is as much to say, as a clear

equal

:qual voice : or as *Golius* hath it a word directly and equally cast forth.

J. Golius addit. de Reg. Cath. pag. 4.

The third ＼ answers to MI ; expressing with them of *China*, a lofty voice: more strongly delivered, but more flat in the pronunciation than the former.

The fourth ／ answers to FA, and *Chiniquely* signifies, the lofty voice of one who is going forth; that speaks, in contrary to ＼, more freely and in an higher Tone ; or as if it proceeded from one that puts a question.

The fifth υ answers to SOL, and thereby in the Language of *China*, the quick or hasty voice of one that is comming in, is intended.

The last, *O*, as also, ） denote a plain voice.

By this invention the Society came to be much aided in overcoming the difficulty of the speech: And by the help of these notes strangers learn the Language, but with what labour, and by how many reflexions, is easier in thought to be imagined, than by the pen, saith *Kircherus*, to be expressed. So that it is cleerly manifest this difficulty relateth unto Foreiners particularly; for the native *Chinois*, as the same Author affirmeth, never observe any Accents at all, but from their cradles, as almost all other Nations, are accustomed to the pronuntiation of their MOTHER Tongue, although their *Literati* not only *in actu exercito*, but *in actu signato*, both in the Practique and Theory; know and teach every Letter to be pronounced truly, according to the respective Accent due to it. Which more fully adjusts the simplicity and

A. Kir. Ch Ill. par. 6. p. 236.

O 4   purity

purity of their Language; and the strict care they take to preserve the same.

Now, as this difficulty is great unto strangers, who alwayes in attaining whatever speech encounter much; So they are abundantly recompenced, and more advantaged in other respects; not only in regard as you lately heard, of the incredible commodity they receive, by saving the labour of learning divers Languages, whilst in *China* it self the Idiom varying, and in the adjacent Kingdoms the languages being different, they all agree in writing; but also in regard of the many Elegancies arising from the double sence of the words, on which the difficulty is grounded. For this Æquivocableness is accounted the Elegancy of their Language, which consists, as was said, in the written Character rather, than the vocal word, and there-

N. Trig. de fore to furnish *That*, the *Chinois* neglecting
Christ. Exp. *This*, all their negotiations of what kind soeuer
apud Sin. are transacted, even all their most familiar
lib 1. p. 27 messages sent, by way of memorial in writing,
Pur. Pilgr. not by word of mouth. And from this El·gancy
54. p. 447 it is, that those of *Japan* though they have of late times invented forty eight Letters, for the dispatch of their ordinary affairs, by the connexion of which they express and declare whatever they please. Yet nevertheless the Characters of the *Chinois* in regard of the excellent terms, and phrases their Language affords, either (to use *Semedo's* words) for delivering of their minds with respect, submission, or in applause of anothers merits, are still in such request, and so great estimation amongst them,

as

as that thofe forty eight letters, howfoever they be more commodious to exprefs their conceipts are little regarded in comparifon, but by way of contempt accounted, and called the womens Lettes. As *Chriſto. Barri* a late *Italian* Writer in his *Cochin-China* afferts.

C. Barri in Cochin-Ch. cap. 6.

Secondly *Generality*, Whereunto may be faid, it is a matter exceeding all admiration, that a people whofe numbers of all forts confifts of not fewer than two hundred Millions of foules; whofe Empire contains of Continent at leaft two millions, five hundred ninety two thoufand fquare miles, fhould nuderftand one and the fame Character, and that the felf fame Character fhould be in ufe amongft them. either in M.S. or printed Books, for more than three thoufand feven hundred years. Certainly it feems impoffible it fhould be thus, and certainly thus it is, without fome peculiar care of Divine Power.

M. Mart. Atl. Sin pa. 5.

Neither are their Characters underftood throughout their whole Empire only, how far and wide foever it now extends, and by thofe people generally that were in time either Colonies of theirs, or conquered by them, as the *Japonians*, *Coreans*, *Laios*, thofe of *Tonchin*, and *Sumatra*, with the Kingdom of *Cochin-China*; but feveral other bordering Countries and Iflands alfo, although in fpeaking them, they underftand one another no more than *Greeks* do *Dutchmen*. Becaufe reading the Characters depravedly, they pronounce them in a different manner, *alio atque alio ab iis, legantur modo*, as *Martinius* hath it, which more confirms, that thofe people that read and pronounce the Letters truly, fpeak the
Language

A. Kirch. Ch. Ill. par. 6. pag. 235. G. Mend. Hiſt. del Ch. lib. 3. pag. 140, 141.

M. Mart. Atl. Sin. P. 147.

Language purely ; and that could those foreign Nations read them rightly, they might not only speak the *Chinique* Language perfectly, but also understand one another plainly, in regard the speech continueth incorruptedly in the Character.

And hence it is that *Mendoza* telleth us, that in *China* letters missive ready written and accomodated to all affairs, are publiquely to be sold by every Book-seller in his shop, whether they be to be sent to persons of Honour, or inferiour degree, or for to supplicate, reprehend, or recommend, or any other intents whatever occasion requires, although it be to challenge one another to the field ; so that the buyer hath no more to do, than to subscribe, seal and send them to the place intended at his pleasure.

But their way of writing, is different from all other Nations of the World. For, whereas the *Hebrews*, *Chaldæans*, *Syrians*, *Arabians*, and *Ægyptians* write from the right to the left, and the *Greeks*, *Latins*, and other people of *Europe*, from the left to the right. The *Chinois* draw their Characters from the top downwards, as by Antiquity Hieroglyphicks were accustomed to be written, Their first perpendicular line nevertheless beginning on the right hand of the page. And in their writing they observe such equal distances, that there cannot be any thing more exact.

Thirdly, Modesty of Expression ; for it much reflects upon the *Hebrew*, as to the Antiquity thereof especially, that there are in it many somwhat obscene words ; whereas by all learned men, it is presumed that the PRIMITIVE

Lan-

Language, was an harmlefs and in nothing im-
modeft fpeech; but as innocent as the time in
which it was at firft infufed into Mankind. *Verba*
parùm honefta (qualia in omnibus linguis aliqua) *M. Cafaub.*
de 4 ling.
pag. 28.
objicit Nyffenus, the *Hebrew* hath words fcarcefly
honeft, faith *Nyffenus,* in his objection againft it,
as in *M. Cafaubon;* who had he been acquainted
with the *Chinique* Tongue, might have fpared
his *Parenthefis.* For *Semedo* will affure you, that
the *Chinois* with great advantage exceed in this, *A. Sem.*
Rel. de la
Cin. par. 1.
cap. 11.
for they are moft modeft in whatever they write,
and very rarely in their Verfes (which in all
other Languages are more or lefs lafcivious) is
a loofe word to be found; and what is more,
they have not any Character whereby to write
the privy parts, neither are they found written
in any, or in any part of any, of all their Books.
And from what caufe happily this may proceed,
hath been remembred before.

Under this head we may alfo add, that the
Hebrews are very famous for their honorable
terms towards others, and humble towards
themfelves. As *Jacob* faid unto his Brother E-
fau, Let my Lord, I pray thee, pafs over before his
fervant. Gen. 33. v. 14. *Thy fervant our father is in*
good health, faid the Brothers of *Jofeph* to him,
Gen. 43. v. 28. And, *thy fervants fhall bring down*
the gray hayrs of thy fervant our father with forrow
to the grave. Gen. 44. v. 31. For which the *Chinois* *A. Sem.*
Rel. de la
Cin. par. 1.
cap. 12.
are no lefs famous alfo. The fon fpeaking to his father, faith, his *Young fon,* though he be the eldeft &
married; the fervant to his Mafter ftyleth himfelf
Slave. In fpeaking one with another, they always do it with expreffions of Honour, as
                                                    amongft

amongst us, *Sir*, your *Worship*, and the like. Befides, even to inferior and ordinary people, they
give an honorable name; as, a servant, if he be
grave, they call, *The great Master of the House*; and
we are taught, that *Joseph* termed his Steward,
The Ruler of his House, Gen. 43. v. 16. We read
likewise, that *Abraham* called his wife *Sister*, saying, *She is my sister*, Gen. 20. ver. 2. And, *Take
no care my sister*, said old *Tobit* to his wife, *Tob.
5. v. 20.* And if a *Chinois* speaks unto a woman,
though she be not of any kin to him, he calls her,
Sister-in-law.

In like manner the *Hebrew* is much celebrated, for the mysterious significations of the proper names of men, in which Prophetical predictions were contained; and which *Goropius*
in his *Indo-Scythia*, faith, the first *Hebrews*, might
either by interpretation from the PRIMI-
TIVE Language, or new imposition assign unto them. But though *Moses* might receive by
Tradition from his Ancestors, that in the FIRST
speech, names were thus mystically imposed;
nevertheless, that by Divine Revelation he
might so record them also, there is no doubt to
be made. As; that *Adam* signified *Red Earth*, out
of which he was created. *Eve*, that she should be
the *Mother of all living*: *Lamech*, that he was to
be the first, that should infringe the *Rites of Ma-
trimony* instituted by God, in having two wives:
Phaleg, that in his days the *Earth* should be divided. Now, what these Scripture names may
signifie in the *Chinique* Tongue; or whether
yea or no, they have any such; or how the
names of the Fathers of their first Families before

fore they came to be governed by a Monarch may correspond to them, I leave unto the *Chinique Litterati.* For, to have acquainted you with the affinity between the names of *Noah,* and *Jaus* sufficeth us.

But I am not to forget, that, as in the PRIMITIVE, so likewise in the Language of *China* the proper names of men have mysterious significations in them, *Martinius* in his History and *Atlas* will ascertain you. For, their sixth Emperour was called *Cous* as foretelling the eminent vertue he should be endued withall: *Faus* at his attaining the Crown changed his name and would be called *Vus,* as giving his subjects to understand thereby, what a warlike and valiant Prince, they should find him to be: *Ngayus* would at his coming to the Throne take upon him the name of *Pingus,* i. e. *Pacificus,* as if inspired that CHRIST the true Pacifique King should during his reign be born: And *Chingus* was called *Xius,* which name the *Chinois* afterwards found too truly imposed; for he observed no moderation in any thing, being sometimes vertuous, sometimes vicious, equally valiant and cruel.

Besides not only of their Kings and Great men, but also of all the people generally, both the *names* and *surnames* are significant; their surnames are ancient and unchangeable, and there are not of them a thousand in all *China*; but their other names are arbitrary at the pleasure of the Father. What should I say of the mysterious names of their Empire, having touched upon them before, seeing *Trigautius* tells us,

Purch: Pilgrimage, lib. 4. pag. 445.

N. Trig. de Christ. Exp. apud Sin. lib. 1. p. 84.

Id. lib. 1. p. 4.

us, that it was of old called *Thin*, as being unbounded and without limits; then *Yu*, as the place of rest and quietness; afterwards *Hia*, as much to say, as *Great*; then again *Sciam*, as enriched with all things; then *Cheu*, a place of perfection; but pretermitting others, *Hin* signifies the milky way in Heaven. For, from all Antiquity it hath been customary with them, when any new family came unto the Crown, according to the mystical signification of the proper name thereof, to give a new name unto the Empire.

Fourthly, the *Utility*; for, the Language of *China* affordeth us, the Acknowledgment of one only true God; Theology taught by *Noah*; Predictions of CHRIST in exotique Regions many Centuries of years before his Incarnation: devout Ejaculations, such, as cannot (Oh the shame!) among Christians without difficulty be found; eloquent Orations, such, as nor *Greek* nor *Roman* oratory exceeds; Warlike Stratagems, such, as *Hannibal* and *Fabius* were, and the greatest Captains are to learn: Valour giving place to none; Physick not to be paralleld by any; Agriculture surmounting all: The Mathematiques; Mechaniques; Morality; I cannot have words for all unless from *China*. But if *ex ungue Leonem*, from the claw the greatness of the Lion may be judged; then, for Policy in government, Rules for Magistrates, Lawes for People, not executed negligently like ours (in *Europe*) as if no matter whether yea or no they were ever made, neither Empire, nor Kingdom, nor Commonwealth ever or at this

day

day known, can be brought to ſtand in com-
petition with the Monarchy of *China.*
Whereby, ſince her dominion became ſucceſſive
(the inconſiderable duration of the Weſtern
Tartars ſet aſide) ſhe hath enjoyed the ſame in
a continued ſucceſſion of Monarchs of her own
blood, three thouſand eight hundred fifty one
years, accompting to the year of CHRIST
one thouſand ſix hundred forty four, at which
time the now *Tartars* took poſeſſion of her
Throne.

Fifthly, and laſtly the *Brevity. La ſua Brevità
la fa æquivocà, mà per l'iſteſſa cauſa compendioſa;*
The Brevity of the *Chinique* Language makes it *A. Sem. Rel*
æquivocal, but for the ſame reaſon compendious, *de la Cin.*
ſaith *Semedo.* Whereby we may obſerve, that *Par. 1. c. 6.*
the Æquivocableneſs which is ſaid to be ſo difficult and troubleſome to ſtrangers, is even by
ſtrangers themſelves celebrated; and in regard
of the compendiouſneſs moſt acceptable and
pleaſingly welcome to the *Chinois,* who are very
particular affectors of brevity in ſpeech. Inſomuch
that our Author is of opinion, that they were
either imitators of (which becauſe they are far
more antient they could not be) or imitated by
the *Lacedæmonians.* And elſewhere he conceives,
that *Lycurgus* had his Law for prohibiting the
acceſs of ſtrangers into his Commonwealth from
China. Wherefore, and in regard that *Plutarch*
finds him to have been in *India,* and to have con-
ferred with the Gymnoſophiſts there, we may
preſume to think, that *Lycurgus* during his forien
travails was in *China* likewiſe, and adorned his
Laws not only with thoſe cuſtomes of theirs, but
also

also several others the like , as they are by *Plutarch* in his life recorded, though nothing in relation thereunto can otherwise be collected out of the Histories of the *Greeks*. And why? For that the Lawgivers of the Antients, *Lycurgus, Solon* and the rest, amongst the *Græcians*; as also *Numa* among the *Romans* were too politique, and ambitious of glory, to proclaim from whence really they derived their knowledg; whilst one must have his *Ægeria*, another his *Pythioness*; so *Mahomet* had his Dove, & *Fohius* his Dragon, who because his *Chinois* reputed the sight of that Creature to be a great *Omen* of Felicity, perswaded them into a beleef, that he took the invention of his Characters, and their use, from the back of a Dragon, as it came out of the water, that by a Prodigy the greater estimation might be set upon his new Art. And in like manner, most Law-givers have fathered their Laws upon one Deity or other, the more to confirm the people in an awful reverence of them, and their institutions.

M. Mart.
Sin. hist.
lib. 1. p. 22.

But if the *Brevity* of a Language be a remarque of the P R I M I T I V E Tongue, as it is asserted to be ; the *Chinique* seemeth to surpass all other Nations of the World therein. For as thereby, the Æquivocableness is enriched with compendiousness, so is the compendiousness beautified with gracefulness and sweetness, beyond in a manner all Example. To which purpose *Semedo* proceeds , saying, *con'esser lingua eosi limitata, è tanto dolce, che quasi supera tutte l'altre che conosciamo,* that by being so succinct a Language , it is so sweet, that it exceedeth, as it were all others that

We

ve know. And that we might not acquiesce in single testimony, *Nieuhoff* assureth us also, La *J. Nieuh.* *Brievete de cette Langue est si agreable, que j'oserois l'Amb.Or. resque luy donner le primier rang entre toutes celles par.2.p.13. qui nous sont connues jusques a present;* the Brevity of this Language is so graceful, that I dare almost give it, saith he, the first rank amongst all those that are at this day known.

Now to give a Language the first or *primier* rank, as to succinct *Sweetness*, and graceful *Brevity* is a great step towards the granting of it to be, the PRIMITIVE Language; Considering which, together with the exemplary *Utility*; remarkeable *Modesty*; admirable *Generality*; great *Simplicity*, and high *Antiquity*; we may from these Arguments almost dare to affirm, that the Language of the Empire of *China* is the PRIMITIVE Language. But, having moreover found *Noah* to have lived both before and after the flood in *China*, and that *Their* speech hath from all Antiquity been in one and the same Character preserved in books to this day; which is such a *plea*, as can be drawn up and entred, for no other Nation under Heaven, since the Creation of the World besides; we may more than almost dare to affirm, that the *Chinois* have obtained a ful and final *decree*, for the settlement of this *Their* claim to the FIRST of Languages without all farther dispute.

Now, as for consent of Authors to strengthen our Assertion. It may be demanded, what consent of Authors *He* had, that first found out there were *Antipodes*; or *He* that first discovered the *Circulation* of the blood? Those that so absolutely

P

solutely pin their beliefe upon the shoulders of such consent; are, we may say, like sheep; whither *one* leads, the rest *all* run, without weighing whether the right or wrong way be taken; so that many times they bring not only themselves, but also their followers into errours, who by their prevarication the more encrease them. But what consent of Authors can be expected? The *Scripture* teacheth, That the whole World was drowned; *Noah* and his family being saved only: *Authors* consent, that at the same time *China* was drowned; some few only escaping on a mountain there. The *Scripture*, That *Nimrod* came from the *East* to the valley of *Shinaar*: *Authors*, That in the *East* divers Nations were planted before *Nimrod* came to the valley of *Shinaar*. The *Scripture*, That from the flood until the *Confusion of Tongues*, the whole Earth was of one Language: *Authors*, That from the flood until that *Confusion*, that Language was universally common, as well to *Those*, that were in the *East*, as *Those*, that were at *Babel*. The *Scripture*, That the Language of *Those* only that were at *Babel*, was confounded: *Authors*, That the Language of *Those*, that were before planted in the *East* was not confounded. And all of them unanimously consent, that *China* was planted before the *Confusion of Tongues*; and that at this day the *Chinois* use the same Language, and have the same Letters, as when at first they were planted, and became a People.

We have for many years heard many discourses of this extreme part of *Asia*; many relations have been published thereof; and many learned
men

men conceived thofe relations to be fabulous;
fufpecting as it were the Providence of God,
that any people fhould live upon the Earthly
Globe, in fo great happinefs, in fo great felicity,
fo many thoufands of years unknown. But of
late, what through the unconquerable patience
of *Thofe*, that contemning all difficulties and
perils, have adventured to conquer Idolatry,
and advance the ftandard of JESUS CHRIST;
what through the opportunity, that hath been
given to others alfo, by the late Conqueft of the
Tartars, to hold free commerce in *China*;
we now at laft have obtained, though fcarcely
twelve months fince, the true and authentique
Hiftories of that Empire. Scarcely twelve
moneths fince I fay, wherefore perhaps, as yet
they are not fo much as turned over by thofe
that have procured them. Let them be read,
perufed, and ftudied, and then it will be found,
Authors have fo far confented; That if the
Chinique Tongue be not the PRIMITIVE, I
might, for my own particular, confent with that
great Dictator of learning *H. Grotius,* ” That
” the firft fpeech which men ufed before the
” Deluge, remains now properly in no place,
” only the Reliques thereof may be found in all
” Languages. But finding our no lefs learned
Bifhop *Walton*, and many other famous men,
altogether unwilling I fhould fubmit thereto;
and that *Grotius* was not acquainted with our
late *Chinique* writers, I will now at laft take
leave to be pofitive, that more, and with more
certainty cannot for the fpeech of whatever other
Nation under Heaven, be faid; and that there is

H. Grotius
in Gen.
c. 11.

P 3   fo

so great consent already both of sacred *Scripture*, and unquestionable *Authors*, that we may well conclude, until as full consent, and as great certainty be produced for any other, the Language of the Empire of *CHINA* is the PRIMITIVE Language.

FINIS.

ERRATA.

PAg.5. *lin.*27. For words, *read* viands. *p.* 9. *l.* 12. r. the whole world. *Id.l.*13.r. in the whole world. p. 16. *l.*19. r. Plantations before, as themselves were sent from elsewhere. *Ibid, l.*21. *read* procure. *p.*24.*l.*3.r.*cœlum.* *p.*28.*l.*32.r.*ad hoc credendum.* *p.*31. *l.*14. r.*Judæa.* *p.*33.*l.*2.r. that although those. *p.*49.*l.*15.r.*Chungque. Ibid. l.*16. expresseth. *p.*51.*l.*13.r.*Fohius.* and so in *pag.*52.57.93. *pag.* 59. *l.*24.r.*alcuni.* *p.*63.*l.*19.r. as rich. *p.*64.*l.*2.r.reserved. *Ib. l.*20.r. *Fabius Pictor.p.*67.*l.*12.r. prosecuted.*p.*72.*l.*4.r.*Zaræadras.* *p.*77.*l.*3.r.*ut hunc solum eluvionis.* *p.* 82.*lin.ult.*r.*Tangiu.* *p.*83. *l.* 21. r. in length. *p.*87.*l.*6. r. *Trigautius,* and so elsewhere. *p.*88.*l.*19. r. *ex doctrina a Noe.p.*102.*l.*5. r. their Emperours of old erected. *pag.*106. *l.*15. *Yebiang.* *p.*109.*l.*11.r.Natives. *p.*111.*l.*27.r. *Nanking.pag.* 112.*l.* 24. r. which though many. *Ib.l.ult.* r. *Ucienian.* p, 113.*l.*1. & 20. r. *Sinketesimo.* p. 114.*l.*16.r. *Indico.* *p.*115.*l.* 33. r. *Croceus. pag.* 123. *l.* 31. r. all the Royalets. *p.*124. *l.* 18. r. those Provinces. *pag.* 125. *l.* 14. r. free liberty of conversation and study. *Ib. lin.* 16.r.*Hiavouus. pag.* 128. *l.* 16.r.*Cochin-China.* *p.*153.*l.*15.r.*Kircherus.p.*155.*l.*13. r. *sedes. p.*170.*l.*2. r. decreasings. *p,* 177.*l.*31.r. of the Northern. *p.*182. *l.*26.r. turned downwards.

In the Margin.

*Pag.*78. For, *J. Nieuhoff,par.*1.*pag.*11.r.*pag.*1.Pag.114.r. *Forneux a bois bien bouches.pag.*131.For, *Id.*r.*M.Mart.Bell.Tartar.pag.*1.

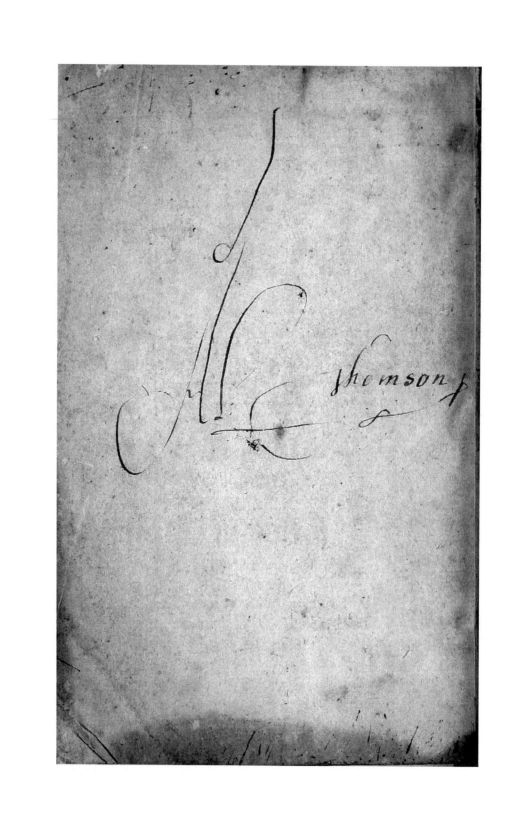

Lightning Source UK Ltd.
Milton Keynes UK
UKHW020635210223
417374UK00006B/790